# MANAGING GOD'S GIFTS

## THREE PERSPECTIVES ON COMMITMENT

# LEO R. VAN DOLSON, PH.D.
# THOMAS A. DAVIS

**Pacific Press Publishing Association**
Boise, Idaho
Montemorelos, Nuevo Leon, Mexico
Oshawa, Ontario, Canada

Edited by Marvin Moore
Designed by Tim Larson
Cover photos by Duane Tank and Bob Michels
Type set in 10/12 Century Schoolbook

Copyright © 1986 by
Pacific Press Publishing Association
Printed in United States of America
All Rights Reserved

**Library of Congress Cataloging in Publication Data**

Van Dolson, Leo R.
  Managing God's gifts.

  1. Christian life—Seventh-day Adventist authors. 2. Bible. O.
Haggai—Criticism, interpretation, etc. 3. Bible. N.T. James—Cri
cism, interpretation, etc. 4. Bible. O.T. Malachi—Criticism, interpr
tation, etc. I. Davis, Thomas A. II. Title.
BV4501.2.V326    1986     248.4'86732     86-91537
ISBN 0-8163-0664-8

86 87 88 89 90 ● 5 4 3 2 1

# Contents

# Preface

The Bible mentions some thirty gifts of the Spirit such as prophecy, teaching, and faith. Most people agree that these are representative of many others that the Holy Spirit uses to bless His church. For example, music is not mentioned as a spiritual gift in the Bible, yet surely those who thrill our hearts with hymns and gospel music are exercising a genuine gift of the Holy Spirit.

Every human being is a "spiritual gifts manager," for each of us receives at least one spiritual gift (see 1 Corinthians 12:7), and most Christians receive several.

Managers must be committed. Spiritual gifts managers must be especially committed. In *Managing God's Gifts,* Leo Van Dolson and Thomas Davis focus on three books of the Bible: Haggai, James, and Malachi. Hence the subtitle "Three Perspectives on Commitment." One of the most important themes of this book is the urgency of Christian commitment, the need for Christians to become serious about using the gifts God has given them—all of them. Not just money but time, the tongue, influence—in short, every aspect of life.

This book was prepared first of all to be used as a supplement to the fourth quarter 1986 Sabbath School lessons, though it is designed in such a way that it can be used satisfactorily by itself. If you are reading this book with the Sabbath School lessons, you will notice that there are 13 chapters—one for each lesson in the quarterly, plus an introduction by Paul Smith.

May God bless you as you seek to become a better manager of all the gifts He has given you through reading this book.

—The Publishers

# Yes! Why Not Now?

"High achievers!" These words describe the insatiable desire and the determination of some individuals to develop highly successful lives. They are determined to be in charge, to be decision makers, controlled by neither people nor circumstances. High achievers will do anything, go anywhere, anytime, and make almost any sacrifice to reach their objectives. They want what they consider to be the "good life," and they are willing to pay the price.

Commendable? Surely!

But what motivates them? Why are they so willing to discipline themselves to the extreme?

Did you ever wonder why some Christians have difficulty relating the idea of high achievement to Christian living? What about you? Are you a high achiever when it comes to living a successful life—guided by Christian principles?

Worldly-wise high achievers often put more energy and determination into serving themselves than some Christians put into serving God. But why not both?

Why not be a high achiever in the management of your life and in Christian living too?

A Christian has an enormous advantage over a non-Christian when it comes to life management and noble achievements. A few paragraphs ago I said that high achievers are willing to pay the price to be successful. Well, that is not exactly the way it is. Actually, we pay the price for failure in the way that we manage life. We do not pay for success. We "pay" for failure. Success produces its own reward in happier, healthier Christian living.

This book contains guidelines for living. You have time, talents, at least some possessions, and a body temple with a mind. What you do with what you have determines whether you are an achiever, live a mediocre life, or become a failure. Our relationship to God and others does not depend on the quantity or quality of our material possessions, nor does our success in life. These are dependent on what we do with the life that God has given us to manage. It is what we do with what we have that counts.

Too often, stewardship has been measured by money and material possessions. But stewardship involves the wise and unselfish use of life—managing all that we are, have, and know, according to God's guidelines for living.

By following God's guidelines for living, you can enjoy success. You do not pay for it. God already has. It is failure that costs. When motivated by love for God, and with the desire for the very best possible life, you can have the full and complete life now. And, through Jesus Christ, you can have eternity too.

High achievement and zestful Christian living do go together. This book will help you to achieve them.

Paul G. Smith
Associate Director
Department of Church Ministeries
General Conference

# CHAPTER 1

# Twenty-Five Cents at a Time

"Most of us would be willing to sacrifice ourselves as martyrs—to go out in a blaze of glory." So said a minister once to a gathering of clergymen. Then he added, "We might liken life to a thousand-dollar bill. We say, 'Take it all, Lord. I'm glad to give all I have for you.' But the Lord answers, 'That's not really what I want. I want all you have—but I want it 25 cents at a time.' Actually," the minister concluded, "it's harder to give ourselves to Christ in little acts of love 25 cents at a time than it is to give $1000 all at once and go out in a blaze of glory."

A quarter is not worth much today. When I was a boy, it would buy 25 penny postcards, or five Big Hunk candy bars that seemed to last most of the day. One quart of ice cream at a store on Fillmore Street in San Francisco cost just 19 cents. You could use your quarter to buy that quart of ice cream and still have enough left for a two-scoop cone. With a quarter to spend you could have a glorious time in a dime store. But 25 cents today is hardly worth what a nickel was then. Thus when we mention 25-cents worth of loving service, we are not talking about a large amount. But a little goes a long way. Precious things come in small packages.

In 1 Corinthians 13 Paul tells us that nothing has much value, not even spiritual gifts, unless it is permeated with love. In verses 1-3 Paul introduces a partial list of spiritual gifts in what seems to be an ascending order of value:

Tongues
Prophecy

Understanding of mysteries
Knowledge
Faith that moves mountains
Total sacrifice of goods
Martyrdom

Then he tells us that without love these profit nothing. Even a thousand-dollar sacrifice like martyrdom, unless motivated by love, profits nothing. But, as faithful managers and stewards of the gifts God has given us, we can accomplish a lot with what we have if we use these gifts in an unselfish, loving way to bless those about us.

The Wolesey family of four new Christians illustrates how little acts of love can make a *big* difference. Soon after accepting Christ they ran across the verse, "If your enemy is hungry, feed him" (Romans 12:20, RSV), during family Bible reading.

"Our sons, seven and ten at the time, were especially puzzled," Elizabeth Wolesey said. "They wondered why they should feed their enemies. My husband and I wondered, too, but the only answer John could give the boys was, 'We're supposed to because God says so.' It never occurred to us that we would soon learn why by experience."

Day after day Dennis came home from school complaining about a classmate who sat behind him in fifth grade. "Bob keeps jabbing me when Miss Smith isn't looking," he said. "One of these days, when we're out on the playground, I'm going to jab him back!"

"I was ready to go down to the school and jab Bob myself," Elizabeth said. "Obviously, the boy was a brat. Besides, why wasn't Miss Smith doing a better job with her students? I decided to give her an oral jab at the same time!"

At the supper table that night she was still stewing and fuming over the injustice to Dennis when his seven-year-old brother spoke up. "Maybe Dennis should feed his enemy," he said.

The other three family members were startled. They weren't so sure about this "enemy" business. They hadn't expected to find an enemy in the fifth grade! An enemy was someone who was way off somewhere. Everyone looked at John. Since he was the head of the family, he would have the solution. But he could only repeat what he'd said before: "God says so."

Elizabeth turned and looked at her older son. "Well, if God says so, you'd better do it," she said. "Do you know what Bob likes to eat? If you're going to feed him, you may as well get something he likes."

Dennis thought a moment. "Jelly beans!" he shouted. "Bob just loves jelly beans!"

After supper John took Dennis to the store, where they bought a bag of jelly beans for him to take to school the next day. That night everyone discussed the strategy to be used. The next time Bob jabbed Dennis in the back, Dennis would simply turn around and deposit the bag of jelly beans on his desk.

The next afternoon Elizabeth waited impatiently for the yellow school bus to pull up, then dashed out the door to meet the boys before they got even halfway to the house. Dennis called ahead. "It worked, Mom! It worked."

"Hey, remember it was me who thought it up," his little brother chimed in.

"What did Bob do?" Elizabeth asked. "What did he say?"

"He was so surprised he didn't say anything—he just took the jelly beans. But he didn't jab me the rest of the day!"

Soon Dennis and Bob had become the best of friends—all because of a little bag of jelly beans and Dennis's willingness to obey God's advice on how to treat an enemy.

"It seems 'enemies' are always hungry. Maybe that's why God said to feed them."[1]

Take a careful look at the text that Dennis and his family found in Romans 12:20 and you will discover that Paul quoted these words from Proverbs 25:21, 22. The context in Proverbs deals with avoiding quarrels. Solomon said, "If your enemy is hungry, give him food to eat; if he is thirsty, give him water to drink. In doing this, you heap burning coals on his head, and the Lord will reward you." Proverbs 25:21, 22, NIV. Perhaps, the heaping of burning coals on an enemy's head appeals to us most. In ancient warfare, those inside a besieged city would sometimes pour fiery pitch or boiling oil on their attackers as they tried to climb the city walls. (Today we are more civilized.

We only use napalm and nuclear weapons!)

The best way to heap coals of fire on our enemies' heads is to be kind and loving to those who are mean and hateful to us.

When we seek revenge, we demonstrate to our enemies that we are just as weak as they are. But when we return good for the evil that our enemies have done to us, they recognize that Christ must be at work in us. This helps them to understand that God can do as much if not more for them. As our enemies feel remorse for the meanness shown to us, the fire of repentance burns up the ill will that they felt. That is how we heap coals of fire on our enemies' heads. They can even become our good friends! And isn't that the best way to destroy enemies— turn them into friends?

That's how little, everyday 25-cent deeds of kindness such as feeding jelly beans to someone who has been hateful to us can make the biggest impact for Christ in this world.

## The Reward Begins Immediately

When Paul quoted Proverbs 25:22 he chose not to use the last part, "And the Lord shall reward thee." But these words carry great significance. The Lord's reward is not limited to "pie in the sky by and by." It begins immediately. Dennis was so excited when he followed the Bible's advice to feed his enemy that he came home shouting, "It works! It works!" But suppose it hadn't worked. Jesus was kind to everyone—and they crucified Him. We may not always be aware of the immediate rewards for our 25-cent deeds of kindness. In fact, many people will not even notice or acknowledge these deeds. But God notices each one, and *He* rewards us with the good feeling that comes from overcoming evil deeds with good ones. Notice Romans 12:21: "Be not overcome of evil, but overcome evil with good." God does not give us victorious characters all at once. By His grace, we develop them 25 cents at a time—replacing one evil trait after another with Christlike traits. If we follow this principle "under the influence of divine grace, every good quality would be gaining strength, while evil traits would as steadily lose their power."—"Ellen G. White Comments," *S.D.A. Bible Commentary,* vol. 2, p. 1017.

"By beholding Jesus we receive a living, expanding principle in the heart, and the Holy Spirit carries on the work, and the believer advances from grace to grace, from strength to strength, from character to character. He conforms to the image of Christ, until in spiritual growth he attains unto the measure of the full stature in Christ Jesus. Thus Christ makes an end of the curse of sin, and sets the believing soul free from its action and affect."—*Selected Messages,* bk. 1, p. 395.

## Commitment Illustrated

When we use the terms *commitment* and *stewardship* in this book we are thinking of much more than financial giving. In fact, material gifts make up only a small part of what God wants and expects from those who choose to follow Him. In His love for us He gave us His all. If we truly love Him, we will respond by putting all that we have and are at His disposal. What we do with the means that He has entrusted to our care is a good indication of the extent of our commitment.

Two stories of giving in the New Testament illustrate the difference between total commitment and half-hearted service. In both instances the parties claimed total commitment, but their actions showed where their hearts really were. Ananias and Sapphira gave much more than the widow who dropped two mites into the temple offering box. But God is never impressed by the amount we give. Two mites given from a heart filled with love meant much more to Him than did the large offering given grudgingly by Ananias and Sapphira.

Peter and John had been arrested in the temple and brought before the rulers for questioning. Finally, on threat of greater punishment, they were commanded not to teach in the name of Jesus and were set free. See Acts 4:1-22. Among the company of believers who welcomed them back were Ananias and Sapphira. The company thanked God for preserving the apostles and prayed for greater boldness in teaching the truth. Suddenly "the place was shaken where they were assembled together; and they were filled with the Holy Ghost." Acts 4:31.

Under the Spirit's influence those who possessed houses and lands sold them, brought the funds gained, and "laid them down at the apostles' feet." Acts 4:35. Witnessing this outstanding display of generosity, Ananias and Sapphira felt impressed to pledge to the Lord the proceeds from the sale of a piece of property. Later, however, they regretted pledging so much. They conspired to keep a large share of the profit for themselves. But because they still wanted the praise that those who gave so generously received from their fellow church members, they pretended to give all that they had pledged. The Lord revealed their hypocrisy to Peter.

To Ananias, who came in first, Peter inquired, "Didn't it belong to you before it was sold? And after it was sold, wasn't the money at your disposal? What made you think of doing such a thing? You have not lied to men but to God." Acts 5:4, NIV. Ananias was struck dead. Three hours later Sapphira repeated Ananias's lies. She, too, was struck dead.

Does such punishment seem too drastic? "Infinite Wisdom saw that this signal manifestation of the wrath of God was necessary to guard the young church from becoming demoralized. . . . The Church would have been endangered if, in the rapid increase of converts, men and women had been added who, while professing to serve God, were worshiping mammon. This judgment testified that men cannot deceive God, that He detects the hidden sin of the heart, and that He will not be mocked. It was designed as a warning to the church, to lead them to avoid pretense and hypocrisy, and to beware of robbing God."—*The Acts of the Apostles*, pp. 73, 74.

Only total commitment is acceptable to God. After we pledge all we have and are to Him, we cannot expect Him to be pleased when we hold back part of ourselves. He who emptied all heaven in order that we might have salvation rightfully expects that we will give all we have in exchange. That is what Jesus must have had in mind when He said of the widow's offering, "This poor widow hath cast more in, than all they which have cast into the treasury." Mark 12:43.

If the offering box in the temple in Jerusalem was anything like the huge offering boxes that can be seen in shrines in Japan and China, the widow's two mites could easily have slipped through the cracks. The size of the coins was unimportant. The heavier coins thrown into that box made a loud noise that pleased those who wanted their generosity to be noticed. The widow's two mites could scarcely be heard. But Jesus heard bells ringing in heaven in response to the widow who gave the Lord everything she had.

That does not mean that God expects us to empty our wallets and purses every time a collection plate is passed. Jesus used the widow's two mites to teach us that what we do with our earthly treasure demonstrates whether our hearts have been fully committed to Him.

## Which Comes First

Which comes first, the heart or the treasure? When Jesus said, "Where your treasure is, there will your heart be also" (Matthew 6:21), did He mean that our hearts follow where we put our treasure or that our treasure follows where we put our hearts? Perhaps He had a little of each in mind. One way that God has ordained for us to develop hearts committed to Christ is through giving our means, time, and talents to his cause. "God planned the system of beneficence, in order that man might become like his Creator, benevolent and unselfish in character, and finally be a partaker with Christ of the eternal, glorious reward."—*Counsels on Stewardship,* p. 15. One specific purpose for the plan of stewardship is to develop greater faith and stronger Christian characters.

But we must not neglect the other side of the treasure/heart relationship. Where our hearts are, there our treasure will naturally follow. Ananias and Sapphira held back part of their pledge because their hearts were not committed completely to Christ and His cause. "It is only when Christian motives are fully acknowledged, and the conscience is awake to duty, when divine light makes impressions upon the heart and character, that selfishness is overcome, and the mind of Christ is exemplified. The Holy Spirit, working upon human hearts and characters, will expel all tendency to covetousness, to deceptive dealing."—*Counsels on Stewardship,* p. 313.

Immediately before making this treasure-heart statement, Jesus had admonished His followers to "lay up for yourselves treasures in heaven." Matthew 6:20. How do we do that? Here is one answer: "A character formed according to the divine likeness is the only treasure that we can take from this world to the next. Those who are under the instruction of Christ in this world will take every divine attainment with them to the heavenly mansions. And in heaven we are continually to improve. How important, then, is the development of character in this life."—*Christ's Object Lessons,* p. 332.

The only treasure that we can *take* with us is our characters. But there is something that we can send on ahead—stars for our crowns. The results of our giving and our service will be seen in those who have been saved as a result.

We should note one other interesting point about this last means of laying up treasure in heaven. As we share what little we have with those about us, God blesses us from His store of unlimited abundance in order that we may have the privilege of giving even more. Every soul that is saved as a result of our donations or as the result of our unselfish service begins a chain reaction of souls won to the kingdom. Until we reach heaven we will have no idea of the final result of the little bit that we have done for Christ in this world.

That is the principle upon which His universal kingdom operates—as we give, we gain. His love reflected in us leads to a great chain reaction of benevolence. A character that reflects His love and benevolence is the one treasure that we can take with us into the kingdom to come. Our greatest need is a revival of true godliness among us. That revival *must* begin soon. It *will* begin soon. Someday we will reflect the character of Christ fully. Why not now? Why not in me? Why not?

1. Adapted from *Pulpit Helps,* April 1985, pp. 2-4, published by AMA International, Chattanooga TN 37422.

**CHAPTER 2**

# First Things Last?

A hundred years ago an article appeared in the *Review and Herald* with this familiar statement: "A revival of true godliness among us is the greatest and most urgent of all our needs. To seek this should be our first work."—*Review and Herald,* March 22, 1887. What can we say? How can we explain this incredible time lapse? How can we as a church justify letting so many other urgent needs crowd out this most important priority? How can we as individuals continue to ignore the implication that, if we do not now make a revival of true godliness the number one priority in our lives, nothing else we do for the Lord can be expected to accomplish much?

All of us are busy. Most of us are busy doing what we have to do to make a living. Some are busy keeping the machinery of a growing, worldwide church running as smoothly as possible. Others are doing the many good things necessary to keep their local churches growing. All of this is good. But it is not good enough! Why? The answer can be found in a careful study of Ellen White's *Review and Herald* article mentioned above. You will find it published in *Selected Messages,* book 1, pages 121-127. If you have access to that volume, please read the entire chapter for yourself, as we can only touch on a few highlights here. It is one of the most important messages available to the church today.

The lead statement of this Ellen White article is quoted in the first paragraph of this chapter. Immediately following that lead statement, she admonishes: "There must be earnest effort

to obtain the blessing of the Lord, not because God is not willing to bestow His blessing upon us, but because we are
unprepared to receive it. Our heavenly Father is more willing
to give His Holy Spirit to them that ask Him, than are earthly
parents to give good gifts to their children. But it is our work,
by confession, humiliation, repentance, and earnest prayer, to
fulfill the conditions upon which God has promised to grant us
His blessing."—*Selected Messages,* bk. 1, p. 121.

"Conditions," "earnest effort," "our work"—some prefer to
avoid that kind of language. But there it is. If we are to have
that revival of true godliness that alone can fill our greatest
need, we *must* meet the conditions. How? Let Ellen White in-
terpret herself.

**Confession.** Much of Ellen White's outstanding *Review* article about a revival of true godliness centers on confession. Confession of sins, of unbelief, of doubts expressed, of darkness
cherished, of a lack of self-control. She mentions divisions and
bitter dissensions among church members—"dissensions which
would disgrace any worldly community."—*Ibid.,* p. 123. Satan
does everything possible to encourage such divisions. When we
yield to his subversive activity, "Worldlings look on, and
jeeringly exclaim, 'Behold how these Christians hate one another! If this is religion, we do not want it.' " *Ibid.*

But there is an even more compelling reason for us to confess
our sins to God and our faults to one another: "In 1844 our great
High Priest entered the most holy place of the heavenly sanctuary, to begin the work of the investigative judgment. The cases
of the righteous dead have been passing in review before God.
When that work shall be completed, judgment is to be pronounced upon the living. How precious, how important are
these solemn moments! Each of us has a case pending in the
court of heaven. We are individually to be judged according to
the deeds done in the body. In the typical service, when the
work of atonement was performed by the high priest in the
most holy place of the earthly sanctuary, the people were required to afflict their souls before God, and confess their sins,
that they might be atoned for and blotted out. Will any less be
required of us in this antitypical day of atonement, when

Christ in the sanctuary above is pleading in behalf of His people, and the final, irrevocable decision is to be pronounced upon every case?"—*Ibid.*, p. 125.

**Humiliation.** This does not mean that God wants to "put us down" or embarrass us. To the contrary, He wants us to have a sense of pride in what we are *in and through Him.* "Alas, what pride is prevailing in the church, what hypocrisy, what deception, what love of dress, frivolity, and amusement, what desire for the supremacy! All these sins have clouded the mind, so that eternal things have not been discerned."—*Ibid.*, p. 125. Considering what the church is and what we church members are today compared to what God says He has made possible for us, "We have not the first reason for self-congratulation and self-exaltation."—*Ibid.*, p. 126.

What is the remedy? "If we are intent upon searching our own hearts, putting away our sins, and correcting our evil tendencies, our souls will not be lifted up unto vanity; we shall be distrustful of ourselves, having an abiding sense that our sufficiency is of God."—*Ibid.*, p. 122.

**Repentance.** Revival is an individual work. As indicated in the passage just cited, each of us must search "our own hearts, putting away our sins." Ellen White spells this out in specific detail: "We must enter upon the work individually. We must pray more, and talk less."—*Ibid.* Just being sorry for sins is not enough. "We must seek the Lord with true penitence; we must with deep contrition of soul confess our sins, that they may be blotted out."—*Ibid.*, p. 125. True confession includes a willingness to forsake sin. "We must remove every obstacle. Let us confess and forsake every sin, that the way of the Lord may be prepared, that He may come into our assemblies and impart His rich grace. The world, the flesh, and the devil must be overcome."—*Ibid.*, p. 123.

**Earnest Prayer.** At the center of this entire experience must be earnest, Spirit-led prayer. "The church must arouse to action. The Spirit of God can never come in until she prepares the way. There should be earnest searching of heart. There should be united, persevering prayer, and through faith a claiming of the promises of God. There should be, not a clothing of the body with sackcloth, as in ancient times, but a deep humiliation of soul."—*Ibid.*, p. 126.

### "Consider Your Ways"

We have discussed at some length Ellen White's outstanding *Review and Herald* article that points out our greatest need and our most urgent priority. It presents a demanding challenge to the church today. It is not difficult for us to dream up excuses for giving priority to everything except that which demands first priority. A classic example jumps out from the first chapter of the book of Haggai.

Haggai, along with Jonah and several other prophetic books of the Old Testament, was written in the form of narrative prophecy. Although Haggai gave his five messages in quick succession in about three months' time, they outline one of the most successful of Old Testament ministries. Haggai means "festive," a name that seems appropriate in light of the rejoicing that marks his brief but most effective ministry.

The Lord's work all too often suffers from the neglect of those promoting it. The first verse of this book tells us that the message came from God through Haggai to Zerubbabel, the governor, and Joshua, the high priest. Haggai directed his messages primarily to the church leaders of his day. That leads to the conclusion that these messages have special meaning for church leaders today.

In verse 2, God echoes the excuse that seems to have won the day among both leaders and people. They were convinced that "the time is not come, the time that the Lord's house should be built." When were they saying this? In 520/519 B.C. Contrast this attitude with the fact that the seventy-year captivity predicted by Jeremiah ended about seventeen years before, when Cyrus issued a decree that the Jews should return to Jerusalem and rebuild the house of God. See Ezra 1:1-4. Ezra 3 relates that the first thing the Jews did on returning to Jerusalem was to erect the altar of burnt offering and lay the foundation of the temple. Samaritan opposition to rebuilding the temple became fierce. They "weakened the hands of the people of Judah, and troubled them in building, and hired counsellors against them, to frustrate their purpose." Ezra 4:4, 5. Apparently these counselors influenced Cyrus against the project in Jerusalem. But Heaven was with the builders. Daniel 10 tells the remarkable behind-the-scenes story of how Christ and Gabriel worked on the heart of Cyrus to keep the forces of the enemy in check.

"This was a time of wonderful opportunity for the Jews. The highest agencies of heaven were working on the hearts of kings, and it was for the people of God to labor with the utmost activity to carry out the decree of Cyrus. They should have spared no effort to restore the temple and its services, and to re-establish themselves in their Judean homes. But in the day of God's power many proved unwilling. The opposition of their enemies was strong and determined, and gradually the builders lost heart. Some could not forget the scene at the laying of the cornerstone, when many had given expression to their lack of confidence in the enterprise. And as the Samaritans grew more bold, many of the Jews questioned whether, after all, the time had come to rebuild. The feeling soon became widespread. Many of the workmen, discouraged and disheartened, returned to their homes to take up the ordinary pursuits of life.

"During the reign of Cambyses the work on the temple progressed slowly. And during the reign of the false Smerdis (called Artaxerxes in Ezra 4:7) the Samaritans induced the unscrupulous impostor to issue a decree forbidding the Jews to rebuild the temple and city. For over a year the temple was neglected and well-nigh forsaken."—*Prophets and Kings,* pp. 572, 573.

This was the condition when Darius Hystaspes came to the throne. The old prophet Haggai, and his younger colleague Zechariah, brought a message of rebuke and hope in order to stir the Jews up to finish their task. Misinterpreting the beginning date of the seventy-year prophecy, the Jews had found an excuse for claiming that it was not yet time to rebuild the temple. God's answer set the record straight: "Is it a time for you yourselves to be living in your paneled houses, while this house remains a ruin?" Haggai 1:4, NIV.

Twice, in a very clear way, God challenged the people to consider their ways—to stop and take a look at what really was happening. Because they had neglected their number one priority, God did not allow what they were doing to prosper. In fact, verse 11 tells us that God called for a drought and consequent famine. The fact that the punishment was more than a natural happenstance was seen in its extent. It affected:

| | |
|---|---|
| their fields | the mountains |
| the grain | the wine |
| the oil | men |
| cattle | the labor of their hands. |

In fact, what little harvest they were able to bring in from the fields, God said, "I blew away." Why? "Because of my house, which remains a ruin, while each of you is busy with his own house." Verse 9, NIV.

In a time of great urgency they were caught up in a Laodicean sleeping sickness—unaware of their neglect. We cannot escape the strong implications that this first message has for God's church today. Caught up in our own priorities, we neglect God's. But His challenge comes through loud and clear: "Consider your ways." It is long past time for us to begin daring for God rather than dozing, as Laodiceans are pictured doing.

## Daring Not Dozing

A group of pious Protestant monks in France chose for themselves the motto, "Do not be afraid to precede the dawn." When I first heard this it struck me that their motto would make a most appropriate theme for a sermon. I proceeded to put one together, abbreviating the title to "Dare to precede the dawn!"

I was astounded to see the way the title turned out on the printed bulletin when I presented this sermon to the Napa, California, church. Typographical errors are sometimes amusing, although seldom significant. This one seemed to fall in the significant category. One letter had been changed in the initial word so that the title read "*Daze* to precede the dawn."

Our country, our world, and sometimes even our church seem to be caught up in the daze that will precede the dawn of eternity.

Statesmen and politicians seem paralyzed by events. The world no longer responds to the political manipulations that once kept events well within bounds. And the churches today seem to be in the same state. The majority are bankrupt, as far as meeting the needs of people are concerned. Consequently, many people are turning to cults in a desperate search for something they can hold on to.

Times such as these challenge us to heroic efforts. To continue to live and work for the Lord in the same way that we have been doing simply is not good enough! It is time to *dare* great things for God. In fact, it is long past time to do so. There is an urgent need to recover from our Laodicean sleeping sickness and address ourselves wholeheartedly to the challenge of our unfinished task.

What can we do that we are not doing? One of the most significant changes we might make would be to rededicate the means that God has given us to meeting the challenges and opportunities that confront us on every hand.

Are you aware that many young men who trained for the ministry are not being hired because of a lack of funds? Do you know that untold opportunities for witnessing are being passed by daily in our large urban centers for lack of funds and workers? Did you know that our denominational presses often stand idle because our literature is not being distributed like the leaves of autumn? And that as a result our publications cost more than they otherwise would?

What about the missionaries who feel overwhelmed by the tremendous demands that they face each day because they have so little with which to carry on their work? What about young people struggling to meet the cost of education in order to prepare for a place in God's work? What about the unentered territories? And what of the millions not being touched by our work in those territories that we entered long ago?

There is so much to do and so little to do it with. If ever there was a time for sacrificial giving and a simplified lifestyle to support it, it is now.

Consider the example of the Eastminster Presbyterian church in Wichita, Kansas. That suburban church began the year 1976 with a construction program totaling $525,000. Then an earthquake struck Guatemala destroying thousands of homes and scores of churches. Eastminster's board of elders met shortly after that, when one of the elders asked, "How can we set out to buy an ecclesiastical Cadillac when our brothers and sisters in Guatemala just lost their Volkswagen?"

The elders voted a dramatic change of plans. They cut their building program to $180,000, sending their pastor and two elders to Guatemala to survey the needs. On their return they recommended, and voted, to borrow $120,000 from a local bank in order to rebuild twenty-six Guatemalan churches and twenty-eight Guatemalan pastors' homes.

The last few years have brought tremendous growth to Eastminster—in spiritual vitality, concern for missions and, yes, in attendance and budget as well. Ronald Snider, who tells this story, reports, "I talked recently with Dr. Frank Kik, Eastminster's pastor. Eastminster is staying in close touch with church developments in Central America and has recently pledged $40,000 to an evangelical seminary there. Dr. Kik told me that their building program to share with needy sisters and brothers in Guatemala meant far more to Eastminster Presbyterian than to Guatemala."[1]

Volkswagens instead of Cadillacs! That is not a bad motto for Adventists to adopt on a personal basis, in light of the challenges that confront us in this disintegrating world. Is it not time for Adventists to *dare* rather that to *doze?*

## A Prophet of Hope

When the Jews heeded Haggai's challenge to dare and not doze, the old prophet became the prophet of hope. The result was spectacular. The thrilling response to his challenge holds out great promise to us today. The 45,000-member "remnant church" that had returned to Jerusalem recognized Haggai and Zechariah as God's messengers. They recognized the truth and the common sense of the message. They immediately began to do something about it. As soon as the leaders and the people began to obey, the tenor of God's messages changed from rebuke to encouragement. Instead of long explanations, God this time sent a message through Haggai, "I am with you." Verse 13.

They soon learned that when God was with them no one could stand against them. They still were harassed by the Samaritans and others. While the rebuilding was going on with renewed determination, some provincial officers visited Jerusalem and asked who had authorized the rebuilding. The Jews told them about Cyrus' decree many years earlier, ordering the rebuilding of their temple. The officers sent a letter to Darius asking him to verify in the royal records whether Cyrus had given such an order. Finding the decree, Darius commanded the provincial officers to allow the Jews to continue their work. He issued a new decree requiring them to provide assistance to the Jews in their work. See Ezra 6:8-12.

Because of His interest in our ultimate well-being, God often allows hardship to come in order to make us aware of our apathy and indifference to the finishing of His work. We cannot expect God's blessing upon inactivity or disobedience. But when we recognize what we are doing and reform our ways, God will pour out His blessing on us. Our blessing and happiness depend on conformity to God's law of life for the universe.

## The Fifth Happiness

Can you imagine a teacher in His right mind insisting to a large audience, "Happy are the beggarly poor"; "Happy are those that mourn"; "Happy are the meek and submissive"; and "Happy are the hungry and thirsty"?

Those were shocking statements in Jesus' day. They ran absolutely contrary to the teaching of the learned scholar and the philosophy of the practical businessman. They still do! Only the spiritually-minded can appreciate their deep significance.

Jesus set forth in clearest terms what it means to become sons and daughters of God. In order to be a part of the family of the universe and break away from the dominion of sin and death, we must practice an entirely different philosophy of life.

It begins with *the first beatitude*—happy are those who recognize their spiritual poverty, for this is the first step into the kingdom of heaven.

*The second*—happy are those who mourn for their personal sins and the evil that characterizes this sinful world, for they will be comforted with forgiveness and the hope of a better world. To mourn is to repent, and to repent is to be comforted with the assurance of forgiveness and salvation.

*The third*—happy are those who deny self and submit fully to the will of God, for they become joint heirs with Christ. Everything on earth already belongs to them, as it does to Him.

*The fourth*—happy are those who continually crave Christ's righteousness, the justification and sanctification He makes possible. The more they crave, the more they will be satisfied from wells that never run dry.

*The fifth*—Then comes the fifth happiness. More than the spirit of mercy or forgiveness is intended here. When Christ dwells in our hearts abundantly, they overflow with His beneficence. We share the blessings received with those about us. Thus begins a chain of mercy and benevolence that becomes God's means for developing Christlike children to fill Christ's kingdom.

To paraphrase Jesus' words: "Happy are those who are so filled with the blessings and righteousness of God that they cannot help but share these with all about them. To give is to gain. The more they share, the more they receive."

This is the law of life for the universe. All things give and, as they give, they gain. This great circuit of beneficence operates everywhere in nature, throughout God's universe, except in the selfish heart of sinful human beings.

Those who operate within this circuit of love continually receive and generously serve. In doing so they partake of the blessing—the happiness—that Jesus promised.

This blessing involves the whole person, physically, mentally, and spiritually. "If the mind is free and happy, from a consciousness of right doing and a sense of satisfaction in causing happiness to others, it creates a cheerfulness that will react upon the whole system, causing a freer circulation of the blood and a toning up of the entire body. The blessing of God is a healing power, and those who are abundant in benefiting others will realize that wondrous blessing in both heart and life."—*Counsels on Health,* p. 28.

Now for the bottom line to this blessing. What about each one of us? The blessing does not come from forcing ourselves to give and share because we feel that doing so is our Christian duty. In fact, such motivation is counterproductive.

Because there is a progressive sequence in the Beatitudes that reflects our growing Christian experience (see *Thoughts From the Mount of Blessing,* p. 13), the happiness of the fifth beatitude is the natural outworking of "the love of God . . . shed abroad in our hearts." Romans 5:5.

This means that, when God's Spirit has led us through the steps outlined in the first four beatitudes, the fifth happiness will follow naturally. Hearts filled with love and gratitude for all that God has done will gladly share their blessings with those about them and in support of Christ's work.

The grand principle involved explains why the best thing we can do with our lives is to commit them fully to God's will. Ellen White calls this great principle "the law of life for earth and heaven." It is one of the great laws that cannot fail. "There is nothing, save the selfish heart of man, that lives unto itself. No bird that cleaves the air, no animal that moves upon the ground, but ministers to some other life. There is no leaf of the forest, or lowly blade of grass, but has its ministry. . . . The flowers breathe fragrance and unfold their beauty in blessing to the world. . . . The ocean, itself the source of all our springs and fountains, receives the streams from every land, but takes to give. The mists ascending from its bosom fall in showers to water the earth, that it may bring forth and bud."

"But turning from all lesser representations, we behold God in Jesus. Looking unto Jesus we see that it is the glory of our God to give. . . . All things Christ received from God, but He took to give. So in the heavenly courts, in this ministry for all created beings: through the beloved Son, the Father's life flows out to all; through the Son it returns, in praise and joyous service, a tide of love, to the great Source of all."—*The Desire of Ages,* pp. 20, 21.

In the same reference, Ellen White calls this law of life the great "circuit of beneficence." She states: "Thus through Christ the circuit of beneficence is complete, representing the character of the great Giver, the law of life."

This magnificent law controls and guides all life throughout the universe. Above all, it involves God on His throne. And it involves us in our day-to-day activities. Its implications to what we are doing with our lives are enormous.

Consider once again that a revival of true godliness among us is our greatest need. That revival *must* begin soon. It *will* begin soon. Then ask yourself: Why not now? Why not with me? Why not?

1. Ronald J. Snider, ed., *Living More Simply* (Downers Grove, Ill.: Inter-Varsity Press, 1980), pp. 12, 13.

# CHAPTER 3

# The Carrot Follows the Stick

If you had to be placed under the discipline of the carrot and the stick, you would no doubt prefer that the use of the carrot outnumber the use of the stick by a ratio of four to one rather than the other way around! If we divide the book of Haggai into five messages, we discover that God used the stick once, and the carrot four times. The initial message of warning to the Jews urging them to consider their ways came as a much-needed rebuke. Once they began doing what they knew they should, God did not just say, "Well, that's fine. It's about time you woke up and started doing what I asked." He encouraged them to continue the good work that they had begun.

His second message was brief but much to the point: "I am with you." They soon began to see that He was. But still a few were not quite sure. They had seen Solomon's temple. Comparing the temple now under construction with the magnificent temple they had seen in their youth, they felt keenly disappointed. This new little temple could not begin to compare with Solomon's.

So God sent a third message, and again He repeated the words, "I am with you." Then He dealt with the specific problem. In essence God told them, "What you build now may seem small compared with the previous temple, but you are doing the best you can with what you have. I am with you. Actually, this little temple will turn out to be more glorious than the former one because the Desire of all nations will come and fill this house with glory."

Ellen White explained what God meant by that promise: "The second temple had not equaled the first in magnificence; nor was it hallowed by those visible tokens of the divine presence which pertained to the first temple. There was no manifestation of supernatural power to mark its dedication. No cloud of glory was seen to fill the newly erected sanctuary. No fire from heaven descended to consume the sacrifice upon its altar. The Shekinah no longer abode between the cherubim in the most holy place; the ark, the mercy seat, and the tables of testimony were not to be found therein. No voice sounded from heaven to make known to the inquiring priest the will of Jehovah.

". . . The second temple was not honored with the cloud of Jehovah's glory, but with the living presence of One in whom dwelt the fullness of the Godhead bodily—who was God Himself manifest in the flesh. The "Desire of all nations" had indeed come to His temple when the Man of Nazareth taught and healed in the sacred courts. In the presence of Christ, and in this only, did the second temple exceed the first in glory."—*The Great Controversy*, p. 24.

This third message to Haggai has a special meaning for us today. "For thus saith the Lord of hosts; Yet once, it is a little while, and I will shake the heavens, and the earth, and the sea, and the dry land; and I will shake all nations, and the desire of all nations shall come." Haggai 2:6, 7. The apostle Paul quotes this passage in Hebrews 12:26, 27: "Whose voice then shook the earth: but now he hath promised, saying, Yet once more I shake not the earth only, but also heaven. And this word, Yet once more, signifieth the removing of those things that are shaken, as of things that are made, that those things which cannot be shaken may remain."

Hebrews applies this text from Haggai to the second coming of Christ rather than to the first. At the time of earth's final shaking, whatever can be removed in this world of sin will be removed. "When God's voice again shakes heaven and earth only that which is right and pure and true will remain."— *S.D.A. Bible Commentary*, vol. 7, p. 488.

In a sense, that shaking of all nations has begun already. If we pay attention to the events around us, we will hear the tread of Heaven's army along the pathway of time. Soon the world will be filled with the presence of the Desire of all nations— Jesus, our coming King. Soon it will be more true than ever before that "in this place will I give peace, saith the Lord of hosts." Haggai 2:9.

## "Satisfied With His Presence"

But before we are ready for eternal peace, we must allow the Desire of all nations to come into the temple of our hearts in order that His glory can fill our lives and be seen in our witness.

Nothing in life can compare with knowing Jesus. The entire Bible contains the "testimony of Jesus." It calls attention to the restlessness that fills the hearts of those who have not become acquainted with our Lord, testifying to the peace and assurance that come from truly knowing Him. It is not enough just to study *about* Jesus. We can learn the facts that surround His birth, life, death, and resurrection and still not know Him as our personal Redeemer.

Christ Himself shared the promise with us that "this is the will of him that sent me, that every one which seeth the Son, and believeth on him, may have everlasting life." "Verily, verily, I say unto you, He that believeth on me hath everlasting life." John 6:40, 47. We can have everlasting life *now*! "As through Jesus we enter into rest, heaven begins here. We respond to His invitation, Come, learn of Me, and in thus coming we *begin* the life eternal. Heaven is a ceaseless approaching to God through Christ. The longer we are in the heaven of bliss, the more and still more of glory will be opened to us; and the more we know of God, the more intense will be our happiness. As we walk with Jesus in this life, we may be filled with His love, *satisfied with His presence*. All that human nature can bear, we may receive here."—*The Desire of Ages,* pp. 331, 332, italics supplied.

What a thrilling promise! How exciting to become better acquainted with Jesus every day that passes—to be "satisfied with His presence." The more we know Him the more we love Him, and the more we love Him the more we will come to be like Him. "Redemption is that process by which the soul is trained for heaven. This training means a knowledge of Christ. It means emancipation from ideas, habits, and practices that have been gained in the school of the prince of darkness. The soul must be delivered from all that is opposed to loyalty to God."—*Ibid.*, p. 330.

When this becomes our experience we find that for which our hearts have been restlessly searching—that which we have heretofore been unable to identify as the object of our search. This discovery enables us to be at peace with God, with those about us, and with ourselves. "In the heart of Christ, where reigned perfect harmony with God, there was perfect peace. He was never elated by applause, nor dejected by censure or disappointment. Amid the greatest opposition and the most cruel treatment, He was still of good courage. But many who profess to be His followers have an anxious, troubled heart, because they are afraid to trust themselves with God. They do not make a complete surrender to Him; for they shrink from the consequences that such a surrender may involve."—*Ibid.* The only way to perfect peace is through complete surrender to God—to trust Him completely with all that we have and are. Our plans, our ambitions, our status, our perquisites and possessions, are yielded to Him because we trust His love and goodness toward His earthly sons and daughters. When we have this confident relationship, we have everything that this life and eternity can bring. Without it we have nothing, even though we may seem to have everything.

"It is the love of self that brings unrest. When we are born from above, the same mind will be in us that was in Jesus, the mind that led Him to humble Himself that we might be saved. Then we shall not be seeking the highest place. We shall desire to sit at the feet of Jesus, and learn of Him. We shall understand that the value of our work does not consist in making a show and noise in the world, and being active and zealous in our own strength. The value of our work is in proportion to the impartation of the Holy Spirit. Trust in God brings holier qualities of mind, so that in patience we may possess our souls."

"Those who take Christ at His word, and surrender their

souls to His keeping, their lives to His ordering, will find peace and quietude. Nothing of the world can make them sad when Jesus makes them glad by His presence."—*Ibid.*, pp. 330, 331.

That is the key. There is no lasting satisfaction in life outside this experience with Jesus. Real peace, assurance, and happiness come from being "satisfied with His presence."

### "Consider Your Ways"

God's fourth message through the prophet Haggai (2:10-19) teaches us that it is easy to be defiled by the unclean things surrounding us. Once again He calls for careful consideration of how things stand. But this time there is a major difference. Before when God challenged, "consider your ways," the picture was not a pleasant one. Blight, mildew, hail, famine, drought— all demonstrated the consequences of self-interest. But this time the people's expectations were to be more than fulfilled. There had been no time for a harvest, yet in verse 19 God asked: "Is the seed yet in the barn? Do the vine, the fig tree, the pomegranate, and the olive tree still yield nothing?" Then He added, *"From this day on I will bless you."* Haggai 2:19, RSV, emphasis supplied.

God was giving His people an I.O.U., which, because it was issued by the God of heaven, was just as good as the actuality. The Jews had reconsidered their ways, determining to follow God's will completely. Now they could be sure that an abundant harvest would soon come. There is nothing in the sacred record that tells what kind of harvest took place, but they did not need to record it. It was good, because God had promised that it would be.

### "Much More"

Haggai's fifth and final message is a message of reward. He received this message on the same day that the fourth was given. It repeats the message of shaking the nations: "Tell Zerubbabel governor of Judah that I will shake the heavens and the earth. I will overturn royal thrones and shatter the power of the foreign kingdoms. I will overthrow chariots and their drivers; horses and their riders will fall, each by the sword of his brother." Haggai 2:21, 22, NIV. The context indicates that the shaking at that time involved the overthrow of Judah's enemies and persecutors. But this prophecy also has last-day overtones. It applies to the final establishment of Christ's kingdom on earth following the final shaking of the nations. See Revelation 16:17, 18.

Another striking part of this fifth message remains to be studied. " 'On that day,' declares the Lord Almighty, 'I will take you, my servant Zerubbabel son of Shealtiel,' declares the Lord, 'and I will make you like my signet ring, for I have chosen you.' " Haggai 2:23, NIV. The temple is not the true seal or sign of God's presence and blessing. Instead, the true sign is a joyful, abundantly blessed people. The glory of the Lord in His people today, as well as in Zerubbabel's time, brings a glory to their faces and a brilliance to their characters that cannot be gainsaid. Thus God's people become His signet ring—His seal. The seal of God is not just something placed externally upon His people. It is to be impressed where the whole universe will see it—on their characters. In that way we become God's answer to the problem of rebellion and sin in the world, not just part of the problem.

God desires to bless us *much more* than we can appreciate. He glories in opening the windows of heaven and pouring out on His obedient people all the blessings that they can possibly receive.

Do recent world events cause you to feel that the world is being overwhelmed with sin and its awful results? If so, take a thoughtful look at Paul's conclusion that where sin abounds, grace *much more* abounds. See Romans 5:20. If this were not so, we might rightfully accuse God of insensitivity to the welfare of His creatures for allowing sin in the first place. But God *is* interested in us and concerned that, even in this sinful world, His children have the very best available. Notice that Romans 5:9-20 contains five "much more" statements.

The first two are mentioned in verses 9 and 10, which we can summarize as follows: If Christ died for us when we were sinners, we can be certain that He will do *much more* for us now that we are justified. Through a personal union with Christ we will not only be saved from the wrath of God but also will ulti-mately receive the joyous fruits of salvation.

Verses 15 and 17 develop the point that through Adam's of-fense death became the rule, but *much more* has been accom-plished through Jesus. The "many" who accept the results of His death and the abundance of His grace come under the rule of life as God planned it originally. Thus "where sin abounded grace did much more abound." It is this *much more* that Paul seems particularly to be excited about. We have such over-whelming evidence of the tremendous love and concern God has even for "enemies" that we can have positive assurance that He will provide every good gift for those who accept His work of grace.

What we need to catch from all this is Paul's enthusiasm. His excitement centers in the discovery that God has far more to offer than we seem to comprehend. Most thrilling is the realiza-tion that He is anxious for us to take full advantage of the spe-cial opportunities His glorious provisions of grace provide. They are far beyond our capacity to ask or think. Particularly at this point in the history of the church it is essential for God's people to receive more, *much more* of Heaven's blessing. Living in the time of the final outpouring of the Holy Spirit known as the latter rain, we have not yet partaken fully of the blessings available in the early rain. They are at our disposal right now, if we will open our hearts to receive them.

If our world often seems to be filled with the tragedies of a sinful environment, we need to realize that this is not what God wants. He has *much more* in the way of the abundant blessings of grace ready to pour out on us whenever we will take time to recognize that what we already have is not enough.

## "More Than Conquerors"

Adding to the "much more" God promises in Romans 5, Paul sounds a glorious, triumphant note in Romans 8:37. There he tells us that by God's grace we can be "more than conquerors." This theme was dramatically illustrated in a story by Ramona Mary Trees in the October 18, 1955, *Youth's Instructor*. She de-scribes Charley Reynolds's conversion. Then she tells how he became a successful literature evangelist. Following a busy summer, Charley loaded stacks of books and his "almost six feet of bronzed young manhood" on a bicycle as he began his delivery rounds.

The first house he came to was that of Mrs. Sanders. She seemed hesitant to accept delivery. When he pressed her about it she told him how angry her husband had become over the fact that she had ordered the book. Undaunted, Charley went in search of Mr. Sanders who turned out to be a burly blacksmith. "There were several loungers standing around in the shop, and Mr. Sanders winked at them as he poured out upon Charley a torrent of abuse."

"A change began to take place in Charley's countenance. . . . A white line drew about his compressed lips, and his eyes blazed warningly. . . . Why, if it was swearing that was wanted! Charley opened his lips. Then he closed them again; and, turning without a word, threw himself onto his bicycle and pedaled quickly away.

"The blacksmith laughed long and uproariously. 'Guess I fixed that young upstart! Cowards—all of them book agents. I'll learn 'em not to come around *my* house—talkin' the old woman into spendin' my good money.'

"For a while there was an animated conversation . . . ; but finally one of the bystanders remarked, 'Likely looking man, though. You know, it seems to me I've seen that fellow before some place.'

" 'I was thinking the same thing,' chimed in [another]. . . . 'That man's face is as familiar to me as Sanders.'

"The first man was lost in thought. Finally he burst out in triumph, 'I've seen him all right—and *so* have you! That's Charley Reynolds, the champion heavyweight boxer of New Zealand!'

" 'You're crazy, Max! Do you suppose Charley Reynolds would stand here and let Joe talk to him like that! . . . And besides—what would he be doin' away off here sellin' books?' "

Max went to get a picture of Charley Reynolds in order to prove his point. In the meantime Charley pedaled to the outskirts of the town and threw himself onto the grass. He was so angry that he wanted to go back and break Mr. Sanders in two with his bare hands. But he was a Christian now. He couldn't do that. Something other than his old nature took control, enabling him to forget those jeering men and to yield himself fully to act as Jesus would under the circumstances.

"Out in front of the blacksmith shop the men were bending their heads over a large picture of a young man in boxing trunks. Their faces were sober now, and very perplexed.

" 'It's him all right, but I can't understand why in the world. . .'

" 'It's too late to worry about that now. Here he comes back again! He's sure after you, Joe; and I don't know that I blame him any.'

"Involuntarily Joe's eyes darted about, seeking a way of escape. It was too late. Charley Reynolds was advancing rapidly toward him. The blacksmith's face took on a sickly, greenish hue. Straight up to the little group of expectant men walked Charley, totally ignoring the fact that he had been there before that afternoon. He wore his broadest smile.

" 'Good day. You are Mr. Sanders, I believe. I have brought a book that your wife ordered from me a few weeks ago. It has to do with the things of God; and if you follow its teaching, you will bring a great blessing into your home.'

"Hastily Joe Sanders drew a rather well-filled wallet from his pocket and counted out the money. His face was a study in mixed emotions. Not a word was spoken as Charley calmly wrote out a receipt, and handed it to the bewildered man. Before he was out of sight, all the heads were bent over the scrap of paper, studying the signature. There it was—Charley Reynolds! Finally Max spoke soberly. 'I guess he must have got religion all right; and all I can say is, it's the real thing. Let's have a look at the book, Joe. There must be something to it if it makes a man act like that.' "

God's character impressed on the hearts and lives of His people becomes the signet or seal of His ability to do much more than we think possible in us, through us, and for us.

Our greatest need is a revival of true godliness among us. That revival *must* begin soon. It *will* begin soon. Ask yourself: Why not now? Why not with me? Why not?

# CHAPTER 4

# Tests and Temptations

## James 1:1-15

The book of James is about the workaday world and the people who inhabit it: The haves and have-nots, laborers and law courts, markets and farms, banks and shops, work and leisure, greed and generosity, self-indulgence and self-control, pride and humility, victory and defeat, belief and doubt, faith and works, laughter and tears, the sick and the healthy, evil and good, sin and forgiveness. We find them all in James, a very down-to-earth writer who nevertheless sees the world, as all New Testament writers see it, in the light of eternity.

James, then, is a man whose Christianity is practical. To him that means prayer as well as action, faith in place of doubt, humility instead of self-glorification. And above all, the glorification of God.

**1. James, a servant of God.** Many commentators believe that the author of James is the brother of Jesus mentioned in Galatians 1:19. See Matthew 13:55. He is so identified by the first-century Jewish historian, Josephus, and by Eusebius, the fourth-century historian and bishop of Caesarea. But there is insufficient evidence in historical writings to be conclusive.

James has referred to himself as "a servant of God" (James 1:1), indicating that he thinks of himself as belonging completely to God, committed to do His will, not his own or that of others. This is the requirement for every Christian.

**To the twelve tribes which are scattered abroad.** Is James writing to Jews or Gentiles? Some scholars hold he is addressing Christian Jews. Others believe that "twelve tribes" is used metaphorically for the true Israel, those for whom heaven is home and earth is only a foreign country. So they are a Diaspora—refugees on earth. The message of the epistle is not affected, whichever view one adopts.

**2. My brethren, count it all joy when ye fall into divers (RSV, "various") temptations.** James begins his epistle on an upbeat note. But is not his optimism strange? Be joyful because you have troubles and trials? A. T. Robertson tells us that the Greek means "unmixed joy." Have joy that is unmixed, nothing detracting from it, because you have troubles! Is that exhortation reasonable?

From a strictly human viewpoint, no. We may accept trials stoically, perhaps. We make the best of a bad situation, refusing to let it get us down. But James tells us to *rejoice* over our trials.

The solution to this enigma is that human joy is experienced in the unstable atmosphere of changing conditions. It has shallow roots. It springs from pleasing situations. It cannot exist where circumstances are not just right. It has no solid foundation. That is why "the joy of the godless lasts but a moment." Job 20:5, NIV.

Christian joy is rooted in a relationship. The psalmist knew this. "In thy presence is fullness of joy," he wrote. Psalms 16:11. So the Christian is joyful because he knows that his Lord is with him and that whatever comes to him is by permission of God and has the purpose of accomplishing his sanctification and ultimate glorification.

Christian joy springs from the assurance that even when the world seems to be falling apart, the Christian knows that God is in control of every atom and that His purpose *will* be worked out.

What does James mean by "falling" into (RSV, "meet"; NASB, "encounter") trials. The Christian is bound to confront unsought opposition and trying ordeals. But *walking* into temptation is another thing. Walking into temptation invites failure. It is occasion for self-examination, repentance, and prayer for better judgment and a more careful seeking of God's will.

**The trying of your faith worketh patience (RSV, "steadfastness").** A Christian's faith must be brought to the test of temptation and trial just as gold must be put into the crucible and the fire. But the fire will not be hotter than can be borne by him who is in Christ. God "will not allow you to be tested beyond your power." 1 Corinthians 10:13, TEV. He who is not in Christ *will* be tempted beyond his power. He will find the test too much for him. But the one who trusts in Jesus will overcome.

Steadfastness, or patience, is the atmosphere in which other virtues grow. Just as a particular crop depends on a certain kind of weather to flourish, so the Christian virtues need a constant perseverance to prosper. When steadfastness fails, the other virtues begin to wither away.

Steadfastness, particularly under strong pressure, is not commonplace. That is one reason why so few will be saved. See Luke 13:23, 24. Only he who is steadfast to the end will be saved. See Matthew 10:22.

**4. Let patience have her perfect work.** The thrust of the Greek is, let patience, or steadfastness, persist in resisting evil and standing up under trials. The possibility of becoming discouraged is implied in these words, so James encourages his readers to "hang in there."

**That ye may be perfect and entire.** *Perfect* refers to full moral maturity, the stage of character development contemplated for the Christian, which is the full reflection of Christ's character. *Entire* means "lacking in nothing." RSV. There is symmetry and balance in the character. Every spiritual quality is present. We are reminded of the fruit of the Spirit (see Galatians 5:22) of which "not one will be missing" in the born-again person. See *The Desire of Ages,* p. 676.

**5. If any of you lack wisdom.** Lack means to be deficient in, to fall short of. Verse 4 speaks of lacking nothing, but then James continues, "If you should be deficient in wisdom . . ."

Wisdom is sometimes defined as the ability to apply knowledge. But James has more than human wisdom in mind. "Human cleverness and worldly wisdom are not only always inadequate but often definitely misleading. The Christian needs a different *wisdom,* a spiritual insight that will save him from slipping back into the follies of the unregenerate man."[1] This is a wisdom that is always in harmony with God's Word.

Paul's treatise on wisdom in 1 Corinthians 1:26 to 2:5 is a commentary on the wisdom James is writing about: "Not many of you were wise according to worldly standards, . . . but God chose what is foolish in the world to shame the wise." Verses 26, 27, RSV.

**Let him ask of God, that giveth to all men liberally, and upbraideth not; and it shall be given him.** The Greek says, "Let him ask continually." As noted above, we so easily fall back on poor human wisdom. We must look to God for heavenly wisdom, or we shall think, act, or speak unwisely even though it may appear good from the world's perspective.

James writes encouragingly. The Christian may think himself presumptuous, or unworthy to ask. But God delights to give to those who ask Him. He gives graciously, according to their need. And He requires nothing in return, except. . . .

**6. But let him ask in faith, nothing wavering.** In context, James means a confidence that God will give what is requested. See Matthew 21:21; Colossians 1:23. Doubting hints at inner spiritual instability from which stem unsteadiness, a fickle mind, and subjection to fluctuating impulses.

**For he that wavereth is like a wave of the sea driven with the wind and tossed.** James goes to nature for a visual picture to illustrate his point. The doubter is likened to the instability of a billow which changes from moment to moment as it sweeps along—an apt symbol of a mind that cannot settle itself in belief.

There are many reasons for this condition: A questioning of God's willingness to respond to prayer, sin in the life, a "wisdom above that which is written," the opinion that such faith is naive, a divided heart, divided loyalty. The spirit of prophecy refers to a double-minded man as "he who seeks to follow his own will, while professing to do the will of God."—*Patriarchs and Prophets,* p. 384.

**7. For let not that man think that he shall receive any thing of the Lord.** Is God unwilling to give to such a person?

No, but He will not because He cannot. God must give His gifts to people He can trust, and He cannot trust the undependable man.

**A double-minded man is unstable in all his ways.** There is a second reason why God cannot do anything for the double-minded person. He is like someone holding a cup that someone else is trying to fill, but he keeps moving the cup around so that filling it becomes impossible. Such people are illustrated by Elijah's challenge to the Israelites on Mount Carmel: "How long will you go limping with two different opinions? If the Lord is God, follow him; and if Baal, then follow him." 1 Kings 18:21, RSV.

**9. Let the brother of low degree rejoice in that he is exalted.** "Let" is perhaps permissive rather than demanding. If the lowly brother needs to rejoice at all, here is something he may well rejoice about. James does not say what he means by "exalted." We may think of Paul's observation that all who are in Christ "are fellow-citizens with the saints, and of the household of God." Ephesians 2:19. An exalted picture indeed!

**10. But the rich, in that he is made low.** The affluent Christian should not hold his possessions in esteem, but should realize that in spiritual things he is on the same level as his more humble brother who needed encouragement to realize his self-worth in God's sight.

**Because as the flower of the grass he shall pass away.** As Lenski suggests, the rich brother "knows himself to be a poor sinner who is saved by grace alone, whose earthly life is only a poor, transient flower."[2]

**12. Blessed is the man that endureth temptation.** The Greek word for *temptation* appears also in verse 2. The RSV uses the word *trials* in both verses. This is probably the better translation. Enduring or putting up with something suggests an external condition over which the Christian has limited control. Temptation, which has to do with the mind and heart, is not to be endured but resisted.

**For when he is tried, he shall receive the crown of life.** The blessing is not in the trial but in the endurance of it. A good paraphrase might be, "Blessed is the person who keeps on enduring under trial, for when he has been approved, having stood the test trials bring to him, he shall wear the crown of life." See 1 Peter 5:4. God *tests* us to reveal the strength of our faith. Satan *tempts* us to exploit our weaknesses.

"It is in mercy that the Lord reveals to men their hidden defects. He would have them critically examine the complicated emotions and motives of their hearts, and detect that which is wrong, and modify their dispositions and refine their manners. God would have His servants become acquainted with their own hearts. In order to bring them a true knowledge of their condition, He permits the fire of affliction to assail them, so that they may be purified. The trials of life are God's workmen to remove the impurities, infirmities, and roughness from our characters, and fit them for the society of pure, heavenly angels in glory."—*My Life Today,* p. 92.

**13. Let no man say when he is tempted, I am tempted of God.** In the first part of this chapter James deals primarily with trials that come from the outer life. In verses 13 to 15 he turns to dangers springing from the inner life—temptation at work on the heart and mind. He begins by cautioning against assuming that temptation originates with God. Apparently some Christians in his day thought this to be so. The apocryphal book of Sirach says: "Say thou not, It is through the Lord that I fell away; for thou shalt not do the things that he hateth. Say not thou, It is he that caused me to err." Sirach 15:11, 12.

Generally, when people try to place the blame for their sin on God or other people it is because they do not want to accept the blame themselves. That disposition was seen in Adam and Eve. By implication they blamed God for their sin. See Genesis 3:12, 13. One of the requirements for forgiveness is that we acknowledge that *we* are at fault, that *we* were wrong, that *we* have sinned. See Psalm 51:3, 4; Jeremiah 3:13. "We should not try to lessen our guilt by excusing sin. We must accept God's estimate of sin, and that is heavy indeed."—*Mount of Blessing,* p. 116.

**For God cannot be tempted with evil, neither tempteth he any man.** God is utterly and absolutely impervious to evil. It can have no contact with Him. This being so, He is incapable of using it as a tool to tempt man.

**14. But every man is tempted, when he is drawn away of his own lust, and enticed.** We tend to think of lust mostly as sexual passion, but the Greek word for lust here is much more comprehensive than that. It refers to any intense, sinful desire, such as the desire for money, possessions, power, popularity, food, drink, and so on. See Romans 13:13, 14, TEV, RSV.

Someone has defined lust as "volition [will] added to imagination."

There is the prospect for sin in all people, the best saint as well as the worst sinner. This capacity resides, not in some covert, mysterious cesspool of the soul that must be thoroughly purged and purified before Christ returns. It is simply the tendency of the sinful, fallen nature that all humanity has, and will continue to have until the great transformation at Christ's coming. See 1 Corinthians 15:51-53. At that time the fallen nature will be changed, the roots and seeds of sin eradicated, the capacity for sin removed.

For now we human beings have natures that are fallen because they have been invaded by sin and made its tools. Our appetites and passions, sensibilities and impulses, have been perverted and misused by sin. These sin-invaded faculties are not necessarily evil, but in their weakness and virtual powerlessness for good, they are easily manipulated by sin. This sets the stage for the scene James describes in our text.

A temptation presents itself to the attention in any one of thousands of possibilities. But this is not sin. The only power temptation has is the power of persuasion. It cannot compel us to sin. The sin comes when we permit ourselves to be persuaded.

Temptation is an appeal to something within us that has a potential for sinful response. Every human being has these potentials, be it a penchant for pride, impatience, outbursts of temper, or biting sarcasm. It could be overeating or eating forbidden things, sexual weakness, desire for money or possessions, status or popularity. The list is long.

The temptation appeals to a weakness, and the seed of a desire is planted in the mind and emotions to respond to the temptation. The desire must be crushed immediately and decisively.

Then there is no sin. But, illustrating the course of sin, James portrays the tempted one allowing himself to be pulled toward the sin. He allows the temptation to draw him. At that point sin has been committed in the heart, for there is at least a degree of surrender to the allurement. See *Our High Calling,* p. 87.

**15. Then when lust hath conceived, it bringeth forth sin: and sin, when it is finished, bringeth forth death.** The RSV reads, "Then desire when it has conceived gives birth to sin; and sin when it is full-grown beings forth death." The illustration is derived from the birth process. The will, surrendering to temptation, yields to desire or lust, and "conception" takes place. The offspring is sin. Lust is the mother of the sinful deed.

An inevitable course of events has now been set in motion, the outcome of which, in the normal course of things, is death—not biological death but eternal death.

We say "normal course of things" because the results James notes are inescapable only if we allow sin to keep on in the life. "The law of the Spirit of life in Christ Jesus has set me free from the law of sin and death." "If you live [keep on living] according to the flesh you will die, but if by the Spirit you put to death the deeds of the body [if you continue to refuse them access and action] you will live." Romans 8:2, 13, RSV.

1. Thomas Hewitt, *The Epistle to the Hebrews,* Tyndale New Testament Commentaries (Grand Rapids, Mich.: Wm. Eerdmans Publishing Co., 1960), p. 41.

2. R. C. H. Lenski, *The Interpretation of the Epistle to the Hebrews and the Epistle of James* (Minneapolis, Minn.: Augsburg Publishing House, 1966), p. 535.

# CHAPTER 5

# Checking Out Our Christianity

## James 1:16-27

We begin this chapter with James earnestly making the point that all good things come from God, who is unchanging in character and evenhandedness. Then James, the realist, gets into areas that, unhappily, are all too prevalent in the human scene: impulsive speaking without sufficient thought, anger and the unfortunate words and actions that often go along with it, self-deception, indifference to truth, and false religiosity, to name just a few. He implies, in the words of chapter 3:10, that "these things ought not so to be" in the true Christian.

**16. Do not err, my beloved brethren.** Don't be mislead or deceived in this matter of temptation. Satan is a master at blinding men in this respect.

Apparently some of James' readers believed that both good and bad came from God. This is suggested by his use of the expressions "Do not err" or "Do not be deceived" (RSV), which were common phrases used by the ancient Fathers as preambles introducing cautions against popular errors.

**17. Every good gift and every perfect gift is from above.** Every good gift that comes to humanity comes from God. Every gift of any kind that comes from God is good. He would never offer to us that which is base. Therefore He does not bring us temptation, because temptation is not for good but for evil. See Matthew 7:9-11 and the discussion of verse 13 in the previous chapter.

**And cometh down.** Keeps on coming down. God, on His own

initiative, keeps giving blessings to all His creatures, to people who serve Him as well as to those who do not. See Matthew 5:45.

**From the Father of lights, with whom is no variableness, neither shadow of turning.** This part of the verse is subject to some speculation, for the meaning is not entirely clear. Most likely, however, the words "the Father of lights" is a reference to God as the Great Source and Originator of the sun, moon, and stars. The statement "with whom there is no variableness, neither shadow of turning" ("variations or shadow due to change," RSV), probably refers to changes apparent in those celestial bodies.

James seems to be saying that from our perspective even the sun, moon, and stars change in position and appearance. Their brilliance varies. But God is absolutely and forever unchanging in His faithfulness and dependability. There is no fickleness in Him. He is utterly consistent. So again we conclude that since it is God's nature to give good things, He would never bring bad.

**18. Of his own will begat he us with the word of truth.** Here we have a contrasting parallel with verse 15. There, sinful desire is described as bringing forth death. Here the word of truth brings forth born-again people. See also 1 Peter 1:23. This reminds us of John 1:12, 13: "To all who received him, who believed in his name, . . . who were born, not of blood nor of the will of the flesh nor of the will of man, but of God." RSV.

God's spiritual offspring are a result, not of sinful allurements but of truth.

**That we should be a kind of firstfruits of his creatures.** The ancient Israelites called the first-ripened portions of their crops the firstfruits. See Exodus 23:19. They were offered to God and were thus sacred, a pledge of the full harvest to come. Apparently James wrote his epistle when the fledgling church was little more than a decade old, and he spoke of the converts to whom he wrote as the firstfruits of the harvest of the new Christian church.

They were the charter members, as it were, a pledge of the great harvest to come.

**19. Wherefore, my beloved brethren, let every man be swift to hear.** James is saying, As soon as you recognize that what you hear is God's truth, whatever its source, accept it immediately without argument. In matters of principle Scripture admits no argument, no debate, but only acceptance and obedience. We have no right to evaluate issues according to our concepts of truth. We must not judge the Bible; the Bible judges us. See *The Desire of Ages,* p. 312; *Christ's Object Lessons,* pp. 39, 40.

**Slow to speak.** James discusses the moral value of human speech at greater length later in his letter. See chapter 1:26; 3:5-8. Here he throws out a quick, crisp caution. He means that we should not rush into speaking thoughtlessly, dogmatically, immoderately, under the impulse of the moment.

Which of us has not so spoken, and quickly regretted it when the damage was done? The classic example is Moses who, after years of self-control, "spake unadvisedly with his lips." Psalm 106:33.

**Slow to anger.** For perspective, let us remind ourselves that the Bible condemns the anger referred to here. Paul referred to anger as one of the sins for which "the wrath of God is coming." Colossians 3:6, RSV. "Let all . . . anger . . . be put away from you." Ephesians 4:31. For "the works of the flesh are . . . anger." Galations 5:19, 20, RSV.

The words "slow to anger" imply that a Christian can control his emotions. Controlled anger is more likely to be righteous than personal anger. Said William Barclay, "When anger is for our sake, it is always wrong. When it is for the sake of others, it is often divinely right."[1] When Paul said, "Be ye angry, and sin not" (Ephesians 4:26), he must have had in mind righteous indignation.

**20. For the wrath of man worketh not the righteousness of God.** The word *righteousness* in this instance means the kind of conduct that God requires. Anger impedes the work of grace in the soul, and it will eventually destroy the fruit of the Spirit. This quickly becomes apparent when we ask the question, When we lose self-control, where are love, joy, peace, longsuffering, gentleness, meekness, and patience?

**21. Wherefore lay apart all filthiness and superfluity of**

**naughtiness, and receive with meekness the engrafted word, which is able to save your souls.** The TEV gives a more contemporary translation of the first part of this verse: "Get rid of every filthy habit and all wicked conduct."

*Wherefore.* Because of this—because the Christian must not harbor uncontrolled anger, he should also put all other sin out of his life through the power of the Holy Spirit. "The expulsion of sin is the act of the soul itself. True, we have no power to free ourselves from Satan's control; but when we desire to be set free from sin, and in our great need cry out for a power out of and above ourselves, the powers of the soul are imbued with the divine energy of the Holy Spirit, and they obey the dictates of the will in fulfilling the will of God."—*The Desire of Ages,* p. 466.

**Lay apart.** As we "lay apart" sin (the Greek tells us that this is a single act), its place in the life must be filled with "the implanted word," and *of course* the Holy Spirit. "If his Spirit abides in the heart, sin cannot dwell there."—*Review and Herald,* March 16, 1886.

*Engrafted.* Other versions have, variously, "implanted," "planted," "deeply rooted." The term does not refer to something inherent in the human heart, but to that which God must plant there. We must accept it from Him and allow it to take root in our minds.

*With meekness.* James exhorts his readers to accept the truth meekly. The word *meekly* is a key word here. Meekness is a quality of the regenerated heart. Christian meekness may question what man says or does, but it never questions God. All men's teachings must be evaluated by the Word of God. This is not always done as it should be. There is a tendency to accept what popular or learned teachers say. "The time has come when we cannot depend upon the doctrine which comes to our ears, unless we see that it harmonizes with the Word of God. There are dangerous heresies that will be presented as Bible doctrines; and we are to become acquainted with the Bible so that we may know how to meet them. The faith of every individual will be tested, and everyone will pass through a trial of close criticism."—*Evangelism,* pp. 590, 591.

**22. But be ye doers of the word, and not hearers only.**
Live your beliefs. These words summarize the teaching of the whole epistle. According to Carl F. H. Henry, "The biblical emphasis is on *doing* the truth,"[2] and he observes that the injunction to be doers, not merely hearers, is actually the thrust of the whole Bible.

Truth cannot long exist as a living thing in the heart that does not develop fruit. "He that *doeth* righteousness is righteous." 1 John 3:7, emphasis supplied.

**Deceiving your own selves.** The human mind can be wondrously cunning at deceiving itself. One way this happens in religious matters is through believing that intellectual assent is synonymous with Christian living. "The greatest deception of the human mind in Christ's day was that a mere assent to the truth constitutes righteousness. . . .

"The same danger still exists. Many take it for granted that they are Christians, simply because they subscribe to certain theological tenets. But they have not brought the truth into practical life. They have not believed and loved it, therefore they have not received the power and grace that come through sanctification of the truth."—*The Desire of Ages,* pp. 309, 310.

**23, 24. For if any be a hearer of the word, and not a doer, he is like unto a man beholding his natural face in a glass: For he beholdeth himself, and goeth his way, and straightway forgetteth what manner of man he was.** A person who only mentally accepts truth and does not try to live it is like one who momentarily glances in a mirror, checks his tie or her hair, then immediately gets caught up with other things and forgets what he saw.

Many situations in life tend to turn even the most solemn thoughts from God. People may be made profoundly aware of their spiritual needs by a sermon, yet afterward greet friends outside the church and become drawn into frivolous conversation. In five minutes the solemn effects of the sermon are gone.

**25. But whoso looketh.** This look is much different from the casual glance of verse 23. Here we see a person bending over something he wishes to observe carefully. He becomes absorbed with what he is examining.

**Into the perfect law of liberty.** The RSV translates, more literally, "The perfect law, the law of liberty." Anciently, even by looking carefully at oneself in a mirror, a person would not get a very faithful image. The mirrors we have were not known until the thirteenth century. Before then, mirrors were made of polished copper or tin, or less commonly, silver. God's law is not like these ancient mirrors that could never give one a very faithful image of himself. "The law is God's great moral looking glass. He [man] is to compare his words, his spirit, his actions, with the word of God."—*Testimony to Ministers,* p. 125.

"As we look into the divine mirror, the law of God, we see the exceeding sinfulness of sin, and our own lost condition as transgressors."—*The Sanctified Life,* p. 81.

James emphasizes that the law of which he writes is a law of liberty, and that is why it is perfect. The idea that a law which reveals the exceeding sinfulness of our sin is a law of liberty poses a formidable problem for many people. How can a person feel free when his spots and wrinkles have been ingloriously exposed? James is speaking about the Ten Commandments. See on chapter 2:8. There is actually no freedom in the law apart from Christ. In Him, the law can give the Christian freedom in three ways.

First, for the converted person Christ brings liberty from the condemnation of the law. "There is therefore now no condemnation to them which are in Christ Jesus, who walk not after the flesh, but after the Spirit." Romans 8:1. Second, Paul makes it crystal clear that Christ brings liberty from sin. Romans 6 is especially lucid. "For he who has died [to sin] is freed from sin." "Let not sin therefore reign in your mortal bodies, to make you obey their passions." "Sin will have no dominion over you, since you are not under the law but under grace." "Having been set free from sin, [you] have become slaves of righteousness." Romans 6:7, 12, 14, 18.

Finally, Christ provides liberty to obey the law. "For what the law was powerless to do in that it was weakened by the sinful nature [subdued in the born again Christian], God did by sending his own Son in the likeness of sinful man to be a sin offering. And so he condemned sin in sinful man, in order that the righteous requirements of the law might be fully met in us, who do not live according to the sinful nature but according to the spirit." "In his own person he [Jesus] carried our sins to the gibbet, so that we might cease to live for sin and begin to live for righteousness." Romans 8:3, 4, NIV; 1 Peter 2:24, NEB.

**And continueth therein, he being not a forgetful hearer.** The person James describes not only looks carefully into the divine mirror to see himself; unlike the one who merely glances into a mirror, he keeps reminding himself of what he saw there. He compares his inward and outward life with the liberating law (see 2 Corinthians 13:5) and is careful to make the adjustments necessary to be in harmony with it.

**This man shall be blessed in his deed.** Blessings without end, now and into eternity, come to those who persevere unto the end to live in the liberty which Christ and the royal law bring.

**If any man among you seem to be ("thinks he is," RSV) religious.** The Greek term translated "religious" relates to public acts of devotion and worship such as prayer, fasting, generous giving to church causes, and faithful attendance at church services, which so often make us pious in our own eyes.

**And bridleth not his tongue, but deceiveth his own heart, this man's religion is vain.** We put bits and bridles in horses' mouths to control them. James compares this to a man putting a bit and bridle in his own mouth. An unbridled tongue is one good indication of a religion that is a shell without content. The subject of the uncontrolled tongue is extremely important, as is evident from the fact that James makes it primary here and also discusses the matter in two other places. See chapter 1:19; 3:5-8; see also Psalms 39:1; 141:3.

**27. Pure religion and undefiled before God and the father is this, To visit the fatherless and widows in their affliction.** This is only an illustration of religion, not a definition. It suggests what religion is, but not all that it is, like defining a living person by saying that he breathes. But a person does many other things besides.

There may be a tendency on the part of church members to overlook orphans and widows. See Acts 6:1. James drives the obligation home forcefully by giving it this emphasis. In American culture there is a disposition to visit needy families with gifts of food or clothing at Thanksgiving and Christmas and to forget them at other times of the year. The Greek here suggests that they should be visited regularly.

**And to keep himself unspotted from the world.** James writes of the world from the viewpoint of the moral evil prevalent in it. See on chapter 4:4. Evil continually provides stimuli appealing to the emotions and desires in fallen human nature. He warns that we must continually guard against permitting this worldliness from applying a moral blemish upon the soul.

Many years ago I read an article entitled "The World's Slow Stain," in which the author reflects upon the insidious inroads the world makes upon a person. He writes of the trusting innocence of a young child and of betrayals and disillusionment that slowly spread cynicism and hardness through the character as the child grows into adulthood.

Worldliness works in a similar way. One spot of worldly influence, not blotted out, never remains as that one spot. Insidiously, inevitably, it spreads like a cancer through the whole character in subtle ways destroying spirituality.

1. William Barclay, *The Plain Man Looks at the Beatitudes* (London: Collins Clear Type Press, 1963), p. 39.

2. Carl F. H. Henry, *Christian Personal Ethics* (Grand Rapids, Mich.: Wm. B. Eerdmans Publishing Co., 1957), p. 132.

## CHAPTER 6

# Faith That Works

## James 2:1-26

In chapter 2 James discusses the attitudes and actions of church members. He stresses that there is to be no discrimination, because all men are equal before God and are therefore to be treated as equals. Partiality, James implies, is a denial of the faith.

**1. My brethren, have not the faith of our Lord Jesus Christ, the Lord of glory, with respect of persons.** The import of this text is concisely expressed by the NIV: "My brothers, as believers in our glorious Lord Jesus Christ, don't show favoritism," or "partiality," as the RSV has it.

The world constantly shows partiality. But we who truly believe in a Saviour who showed no partiality (see Luke 20:21) must repudiate distinctions based on race, birth, sex, or possessions. Despising the poor or those we perceive as inferior is incompatible with Christian brotherhood.

God "recognizes no caste. He places His own signet upon men, not by their rank, nor by their wealth, nor by intellectual greatness, but by their oneness with Christ. It is purity of heart, singleness of purpose, that constitutes the true value of human beings. . . . All who are living in daily communion with Christ, will place His estimate upon men. They will reverence the good and pure, although these are poor in this world's goods."—*Our High Calling,* p. 180.

**2. For if there come unto your assembly a man with a gold ring, in goodly apparel, and there come in also a**

54

**poor man in vile raiment.** James goes on to give an example of partiality. Two visitors happen to drop into a synagogue or church on the same occasion. Their appearance testifies to the great social and economic difference between them. One wears expensive clothing and expensive rings on his fingers. The other is a beggar perhaps, with threadbare clothing.

**And ye have respect to him that weareth the gay clothing, and say unto him, Sit thou here in a good place.** We do not know whether there was such an office as usher in the first-century synagogue. However, James describes someone who, at least for the moment, assumes that function and escorts the "important" visitor to a seat of honor.

**And say to the poor, Stand thou there, or sit here under my footstool.** The poor man is given only the barest recognition and is brusquely told, "You may stand there against the wall. Or, if you prefer, you can find a place to sit on my footrest."

Ruins of ancient synagogues have been found with stone benches running along the walls having lower tiers for the feet of the bench-sitters. This could have been the arrangement James had in mind.

**Are you not then partial in ("among" RSV) yourselves?** When the poor Christian observes the special treatment given the rich man, how will he feel? Does not the partiality shown bring division into the church? Does it not suggest that Christ's kingdom is for the rich and not the poor?

**And are become judges of (better, "with") evil thoughts?** Christians who relate to people this way show that they use false values—outward appearance only—to measure other people's worth. Thomas Carlyle observed that "society is founded upon cloth," meaning that people treat others socially in accordance with their dress. Those who do this bring into question the standards of their religion, which plainly teaches that there are no such distinctions between human beings. God values people on the basis of their inner worth.

Unfortunately the attitude James writes about still exists in the church today—prejudice based on tribal, color, and social lines. See Romans 12:9, 10; Philippians 2:3, 4.

**5. Hearken, my beloved brethren.** James couples urgency

with Christian kindliness and warmth. He says, in effect, "This is a fact you must not ignore."

**Hath not God chosen the poor of the world rich in faith, and heirs of the kingdom which he hath promised to them that love him?** James is not, of course, saying that God has chosen all of the poor to be "heirs of the kingdom." Only those poor who are "poor in spirit" and "rich in faith" are chosen. Yet, while the great majority of those who accept the gospel are poor (see 1 Corinthians 1:26), we must not conclude that all those who are "rich in faith" are impoverished.

**6. But ye have despised the poor.** The RSV says "dishonor," which is more correct than "despised." The term *despise* suggests a hidden attitude. But the one James reproved acted out his feelings, and so dishonored the poor visitor; his insulting actions shamed the poor man.

**Do not rich men oppress you, and draw you before the judgment seats?** When James wrote his epistle, Christians were considered a disruption to society. The rich felt threatened by the Christian philosophy and by the aggressiveness of its adherents who were mostly of the poorer class. So the rich oppressed poor Christians because they were poor *and* because they were Christians.

How strange, then, that church members should esteem one who is an oppressor and humiliate one who is a brother, at least in a social sense. Calvin observed that it is odd to honor one's executioners while injuring one's friends!

**7. Do they not blaspheme that worthy name by which ye are called?** A believer is baptized into the church "in the name of the Father, *and of the Son,* and of the Holy Ghost." Matthew 28:19, emphasis supplied. He then becomes a member of the church family and, taking the name of Christ, is called a Christian. Thus, for that believer to flatter a person who expresses disdain for Jesus, whose name is "above every name" (see Philippians 2:9-11), is highly incongruous and shameful.

**8. If ye fulfil the royal law according to the scripture, Thou shalt love thy neighbour as thyself, ye do well.** The Greek term for "royal law" could mean sovereign law or a law with royal authority. In Scripture it suggests a law that is above all other law, being the law of the Great King Himself. See Matthew 22:40; Galatians 5:14. It is not wrong to show proper regard for a rich man. That simply meets the requirement of the royal law which admonishes, "Thou shalt love thy neighbour as thyself." The breaking of the royal law comes in not showing similar regard for a poor man.

**10. For whosoever shall keep the whole law, and yet offend in one point, he is guilty of all.** How, by breaking one point of the law, does one become guilty of breaking them all, and thus condemned by all and subject to the penalties of all? The answer is simple. Disobedience reveals an individual's attitude toward all law. Thus, in spirit, he breaks them all. Augustine said that the person who obeys when a requirement suits him and disobeys when it does not is following self, not God. James suggests that favoritism falls in that category.

"Whosoever will willfully break one command cannot in spirit and in truth keep any of them. He may claim that, with the exception of what he may regard as slight deviations, he keeps them all; yet if he willingly offends in one point he is guilty of all."—*Testimonies,* vol. 5, p. 434.

Again, it may be viewed in the framework of violated love. Jesus declared that God's law is summarized in love to God and love to man. See Matthew 22:37-40. To show a lack of love in one area demonstrates not only a deficiency in that area, but that Christlike love is not present at all. For when it is present, it permeates every attitude and directs every action. See Romans 13:8-10.

Our text, then, lays down the broad principle that one may not "pick and choose" where moral law is concerned. "We cannot disregard one word, however trifling it may seem to us, and be safe."—*Mount of Blessing,* p. 52.

**12. So speak ye, and so do, as they that shall be judged by the law of liberty.** Make it a habit to speak and do as one who will be evaluated on the basis of the moral law.

Some say that in the judgment Christians will be judged only by their relationship with Christ, or on the basis of love. But Paul, who is frequently quoted to confirm both concepts, also says we will be judged according to our works. See Romans 2:6.

Some people have difficulty correlating law and grace. Augustine showed their interlocking nature: "The law was given that grace might be sought; grace was given that the law might be fulfilled." And Michael Green observes that "healthy Christian living comes when God's commands are seen as the kerbstones on the highway of love, the hedge encompassing His garden of grace."[1]

"How strange the perversion of Christian teaching which presumed that the law of love was a relaxation of the moral requirements of the law of Moses, that the gospel relieved men from an obedience which had proved itself too rigorous for human frailties, instead of what it really is, an enhancement of the depth and scope of moral obligation. cf. Matt. 5:20, 43-48."[2]

**13. For he shall have judgment without mercy, that hath shewed no mercy; and mercy rejoiceth against judgment.** The fact that "mercy triumphs over judgment" (RSV) does not mean that judgment, or justice, is violated. But when Justice finally has her day—as she will—and unrepentant sinners ultimately receive the wages of their sins, Mercy stands by, weeping. But she has done what she could. For the repentant, Justice stands aside in deference to Mercy. So, for the committed Christian, there is no need to fear the judgment.

**14. What doth it profit, my brethren, though a man say he hath faith, and have not works? can faith save him?** James' statement on faith has caused some commentators to disparage his epistle. Luther spoke of James as a "right strawy letter," although he did not reject it entirely. But Paul is showing that works have no merit for justification. James insists that if one has a living faith (which accompanies justification) such faith will work. He condemns that which is called faith, but which is merely intellectual.

Some people insist that faith and works are mutually exclusive, but that is not what the Bible teaches. "God has joined faith and works together; but perverse human nature will insist upon putting them asunder."[3]

**15. If a brother or sister be naked, and destitute of daily food.** The illustrations given here and in verse 2 are probably both hypothetical. The Greek term for "naked" can also mean ill-clad (RSV). Ill-clad is probably intended here.

**And one of you say unto them, Depart in peace, be ye warmed and filled; notwithstanding ye give them not those things which are needful to the body; what doth it profit?** It seems that the term "Depart in peace" was a Hebrew saying, much as we might say, "Have a good day!" However, in James' context it would mean, "May God grant you what you need!" or "I hope somebody will take care of your needs."

To say this to a needy brother or sister would be callous hypocrisy, a mockery on the part of professed Christians who could fill the need but would not.

**17. Even so faith, if it hath not works, is dead, being alone.** Some people are inclined to think of faith and works in terms of faith *plus* works, with works under constant suspicion. Actually, it is faith *at* work. As Paul points out, the Christian is "created in Christ Jesus unto good works." Ephesians 2:10; see also Matthew 7:24. In James' book, faith without works is faith without worth. Such so called faith has no saving value.

**18. Yes, a man may say, Thou hast faith, and I have works: shew me thy faith without thy works, and I will shew thee my faith by my works.** James now throws down an unanswerable challenge to his imaginary dialoger: All right, let's assume you have faith, as you say. But that is only words. I need something more. Prove you have faith! Show it to me in any way other than by works! It does not require much reflection to realize there is no other way.

**19. Thou believest that there is one God; thou doest well: the devils also believe, and tremble.** In what way does this assertion add to the apostle's argument? Possibly as an added point to show that a mere intellectual faith is valueless. Then James would be reasoning this way: The demons have an intellectual belief, or faith, that God is one. But that belief will not save them. It only adds to their misery, causing them to shudder and be terrified at the implications for them. This illustrates that mere mental assent is valueless in terms of salvation.

**21. Was not Abraham our father justified by works, when he had offered Isaac his son upon the altar?** Keep in mind that James is dealing with the *validation* of faith. That can only be done by works, he insists, and he cites Abraham as an example. Abraham believed that God would, through Isaac, make of his posterity a great nation and that, if necessary, He would raise his son from the dead to fulfill that purpose. See Genesis 21:12; Hebrews 11:17, 19. Because of this he was ready to carry out the sacrifice of Isaac had God not interposed.

James' expression, "justified by works" is not intended to mean justification in the generally accepted Pauline sense of pronouncing or counting as righteous. James means, rather, that Abraham's works demonstrated the genuineness of his faith. Abraham's faith was demonstrated, developed, and brought to completion by obedience.

**24. Ye see then how that by works a man is justified, and not by faith only.** Works provide evidence that the "engrafted word" (chapter 1:21) has taken root and germinated. James does not deny justification by faith. He simply tells us that works, or obedience, demonstrates the validity of faith.

**25. Likewise also was not Rahab the harlot justified by works, when she received the messengers, and had them sent another way?** Hebrews makes clear that Rahab's action in saving the Israelite spies was because of her faith. See Hebrews 11:31. It was works springing from faith. She aided the spies because of her conviction that "the Lord your God, he is God in heaven above, and in earth beneath." Joshua 2:11.

**26. For as the body without the spirit is dead, so faith without works is dead also.** Just as the absence of breath is proof that a person is dead, so an absence of the works produced by a living faith is proof that faith is absent, or dead.

---

1. Michael Green, *The Second Epistle of Peter and the Epistle of Jude,* Tyndale New Testament Commentaries (Grand Rapids, Mich.: Wm. B. Eerdmans Publishing Co., 1980), p. 118.

2. George A. Buttrick, ed., *The Interpreter's Bible* (New York: Abingdon Press, 1957), vol. 12, pp. 39, 40.

3. *The Pulpit Commentary, The General Epistle of James* (Grand Rapids, Mich.: Wm. B. Eerdmans Publishing Co., 1962), vol. 21, p. 37.

# CHAPTER 7

# The Trouble Is With the Tongue

## James 3:1-18

Most of James 3 is a discussion of the Christian's use of language—the tongue, as James puts it. The chapter begins with the hazards of being a religious teacher, but immediately generalizes in a broad discussion of the deadly potential of the tongue. James is quite pessimistic. He sees the tongue, for the most part, as a negative organ that gets people into a great deal of trouble.

**1. My brethren, be not many masters, knowing that we shall receive the greater condemnation.** The term *master* may be understood in the British sense of teacher (RSV). James used the Greek term, as it is generally employed in the pastoral letters, of men expected to know thoroughly the doctrines of the church and to pass them on unadultered to others. Being a teacher of God's Word is a noble but serious responsibility, for, as our text points out, a teacher will be "judged with greater strictness" (NEB) than others.

Paul apparently faced a similar problem. In 1 Corinthians 3:10-15 he compared the teachers in the Corinthian church to builders and warned them against using "wood, hay, stubble"—worthless, inadequate, shoddy, superficial instruction. See also Titus 1:9, 10. His caution may also be applied to Christian character building. In times of test and trial, Paul says, the nature of the teaching will be revealed, and then those teachings that are worthless will fail, as wood, hay, and stubble are consumed in fire.

In our day, no less that in James and Paul's, unqualified people are anxious to teach the Scriptures. Some may be unconverted or immature. Others have poor judgment or bizarre ideas. Still others may not understand very well what they are trying to teach, or they think they have the gift of teaching when they do not. These are the people most likely to import "wood, hay, and stubble" to their hearers.

**2. For in many things we offend all.** This chapter begins by addressing teachers, but by using the term "we . . . all" the author quickly turns to his general Christian audience. The RSV says, "we all make many mistakes"—not just teachers and preachers. Literally, the Greek word rendered "offend" or "mistakes" means to stumble, to take a false step. In a moral sense it means committing error, going astray, or sinning. In context James may have in mind, not a deliberate sin, but a tripping or stumbling, resulting from an unexpected situation or an unguarded moment like Moses' sin that excluded him from Canaan. See Numbers 20:1-12; *Patriarchs and Prophets,* pp. 418, 419. A genuine Christian avoids sinning deliberately.

**If any man offend not in word, the same is a perfect man, and able also to bridle the whole body.** James now focuses exclusively on words. The height of self-control, he says, is in fully controlling the tongue. If one can restrain the tongue so that he never speaks unless he has carefully considered, he is a perfect (fully mature) person.

Unfortunately, even the best Christian sometimes speaks and subsequently regrets his words. We are not always aware of the implications of our words or the impressions made by them.

The tongue is not an independent member of the body. It is rooted in the heart, and articulates the thoughts of the heart or the stimulus of the emotions.

**3. Behold, we put bits in the horses' mouths, that they may obey us; and we turn about their whole body.** James now illustrates his point concerning control of the tongue. Without a bit and bridle, a spirited horse will go pretty much its own way. With them, the rider decides which direction the horse will go. Someone has observed that "an unbridled tongue is an unbridled nature." As the control imposed by a small bit directs the whole horse, so the control of the tongue by the will (the logical application of the bit) directs the whole man.

**4. Behold also the ships, which though they be so great, and are driven of fierce winds, yet are they turned about with a very small helm, whithersoever the governor listeth.** A second example adds further weight to James' illustration of the will. The ships of James' day were relatively large. The one that took Paul to Malta carried 276 people. See Acts 27:37. James could not have dreamed of the colossal size of modern ships. According to the *1985 Guiness Book of World Records* the largest cargo vessel is 1,109 feet long and 129 feet wide at its widest point, while the largest tanker is 1,054 feet long (almost three tenths of a mile) and 226 feet wide. Yet the most massive modern ship is still "turned about with a very small helm, whithersoever the governor [captain] listeth." As the captain controls the ship so the Christian must control his tongue. Furthermore, according to verse 2, the one who controls his tongue by the grace of God will be able to control everything else.

**5. Even so the tongue is a little member, and boasteth great things.** Peter writes of those who "speak great swelling words of vanity." 2 Peter 2:18. Here also are "great swelling words"—big talk, big claims.

In this and the following verses James concentrates on the evils of the uncontrolled tongue. His words are graphic and strong. Such language flows from more than theoretical knowledge. Without doubt, during his ministry, James experienced many examples of the destructive force of human speech.

**Behold, how great a matter a little fire kindleth!** As a small spark can ignite a holocaust, so the tongue kindles the whole world in flame.

History is full of episodes in which the tongue was responsible for enormous suffering. Hitler's hypnotic demagoguery ignited the German nation and engulfed the globe in the flames of World War II.

**6. And the tongue is a fire, a world of iniquity: so is the tongue among our members, that it defileth the whole**

**body, and setteth on fire the course of nature; and it is set on fire of hell.** Bible scholars tell us that this verse is one of the most difficult in the New Testament, both because of its tangled word structure and because of the words James chose to express his ideas. A simple outline will help us to understand what James means. In the text we see two interwoven threads of thought. The tongue is:

    1. A fire that
       a. sets on fire "the course of nature."
       b. is itself "set on fire of hell."

There is broad agreement among the various Bible translations that the term, "the course of nature" means something like "the whole course of . . . life," as the NIV has it. The naturally sinful tongue, with its slandering, faultfinding tendencies affects one's entire life and every individual that it touches.

When we think of the years of our lives and the sad effect we know our words have had at times and their life-giving, happy effect at other times, we realize a little better the dynamics of our words and the need to consider them carefully and prayerfully before we speak.

James declares that the source of incendiary words is hell. They are "set on fire of hell." "The fire which inflames human passion and infects human life throughout its entire existence is kindled by the devil and comes from beneath."[1]

The tongue is:

    2. "a world of iniquity."
       a. "among our members."
       b. it defiles the whole body.

This second concept, which James has interwoven with the first, contributes other ideas about the tongue. The term "a world of iniquity" means, perhaps that all the iniquity within an individual is incorporated in his tongue. More than any other body organ, the tongue reveals the evil of the mind and heart. It is the chief channel, the spokesperson, for the iniquities inside the sinner.

The Twentieth Century New Testament suggests what James may mean with this paraphrase: "Among the members of our body it [the tongue] proves itself a world of mischief."

Among the various body members the tongue shows itself to be a vicious, divisive troublemaker. It leads other members of the body into sin, and in this way it defiles the whole body. See *The Desire of Ages,* p. 323.

**7. For every kind of beasts, and of birds, and of serpents, and of things in the sea, is tamed, and hath been tamed of mankind.** The Greek term for "tamed" would perhaps be better translated "restrained," "curbed" (Thayer), or "subdued" (Arndt and Gingrich).

**8. But the tongue can no man tame; it is an unruly evil, full of deadly poison.** James is writing from the human viewpoint. Humanly speaking, complete, consistent control of the tongue is utterly impossible. No man can tame it. It is restless (RSV) as a snake's tongue is restless, darting about. And like a snake's tongue, it is full of poison that diffuses through the whole personality, subtly affecting every attitude, every aspect of life, and the lives of others also. Yet we must remember that the tongue is but an organ to be used. It has no opinions, no biases, no emotions of its own.

**9. Therewith bless we God, even the Father; and therewith curse we men, which are made after the similitude of God.** Some commentators have seen in these verses an indictment of the sincerity of those to whom James wrote. They blessed ("praise," NIV) God, then hypocritically cursed their fellowmen who, by virtue of creation, bore the image of God. But more than insincerity is involved. James knew that without a radical, supernatural transformation, human nature is prone to react to the pressures or expedients of the moment.

**10. Out of the same mouth proceedeth blessing (NEB, "praises") and cursing. My brethren, these things ought not so to be.** We can sense the vigorous tone of protest in these words. How can lips that pronounce the name of the Holy Father in blessing dare to take upon themselves words that utter curses on men? James says, "My brethren, these things ought not so to be." Today we might say, "Brethren, that's not *right!*"

"Ought not" suggests that what *ought* not to be, *need* not be. Whatever God requires He provides the grace to fulfill. "All His biddings are enablings." *Christ's Object Lessons,* p. 333.

**11, 12. Doth a fountain send forth at the same place sweet water and bitter? Can the fig tree, my brethren, bear olive berries? either a vine, figs? so can no fountain yield both salt water and fresh.** These are rhetorical questions. The answer is obviously No. A fountain does not pour out sweet and bitter water from the same opening; the fig tree never produces olives; a grapevine cannot bear figs; a salty spring cannot yield fresh water.

But there is more to James' point than that simple conclusion. A tree or spring can produce only in accordance with its nature. Therefore, if the human tongue speaks words of an opposite and contradictory nature, one of them cannot be genuine. The Revised Standard Version translation of verse 11 suggests which is the genuine: "No more can salt water yield fresh." The spring is really a salt-water spring. Good can never dwell side by side with evil. Therefore, when both appear together in speech, the source is bound to be an evil heart.

**13. Who is a wise man and endued with knowledge among you? let him shew out of a good conversation his works with meekness of wisdom.** James throws down a challenge to his readers. So some of you claim to have wisdom and knowledge. Prove it! If your knowledge and wisdom are genuine, they will lead you to live a good life ("good conversation"). There is a parallel here to the apostle's challenge to the person who claims to have faith (see chapter 2:18): Show me your faith by your works; show me your wisdom and knowledge by your life.

"Meekness of wisdom" means the meekness that wisdom produces. The modern idea of meekness is not necessarily that of the Bible. Bible meekness is not flabby or passive. It is a fruit of the Spirit. See Galatians 5:22, 23. It is found in those who recognize their dependence on God. Thus, Christian meekness is not the docility of the weak but the gentle patience of those who are strong because their strength is in Jesus.

**14. But if ye have bitter envying and strife in your hearts, glory not, and lie not against the truth.** Do not claim to have wisdom if your words, your spirit, and your actions contradict true wisdom. Stop boasting about teaching truth if your teaching is only theory that is not represented in your life. Such boasting shows that meekness is absent and, as the next verse shows, your wisdom is not of God.

Does the term "bitter envying" suggest rivalry between religious teachers? It is interesting to note that Lucifer's "jealous spirit caused him to see many things that were objectionable [in his view], even in heaven."—Ellen G. White, *Review and Herald,* September 14, 1897.

**15. This wisdom descendeth not from above, but is earthly, sensual, devilish.** All wisdom does not come "from above." Some comes from below. The forbidden fruit that Adam and Eve ate did provide them with a wisdom that they had not had before. See Genesis 3:6, 7, 22.

James notes some elements of this forbidden wisdom. It is earthly. It springs from the world's principles, motives, and standards. Its ideas flow downward, away from God into selfishness and rebellion, and conform to worldly philosophies. It is sensual (RSV, "unspiritual"). It springs from the lower, carnal man, caters to self, and can rise no higher than self. And it comes from demonic sources responsible for inspiring false and evil thoughts.

Yet, while worldly wisdom may be devilish, it does not have "hoofs and horns." Initially, Adam and Eve were drawn by its attractiveness; their awareness of its hellishness came later.

Satan knows exceptionally well how to make the world's wisdom appear attractive and the "wisdom from above" dull and unimaginative. See *The Great Controversy,* p. 554.

**17. But the wisdom that is from above is first pure.** James now analyzes the spectrum of heavenly wisdom and offers several qualities its possessor will have. The primary quality is purity, which diffuses through all other qualities.

In the words of the *Beacon Dictionary of Theology,* purity is "a matter of the heart, of present soundness, integrity, and rectitude."[2] "What is pure," writes Carl F. H. Henry, "is uncompounded, free from admixture with sin and falsehood. It shares the straightforwardness and guilelessness of unspoiled childhood, a frankness and openness that has nothing to hide; it is unashamed in openness of mind and heart, and requires no mask because nothing is concealed."[3] Thus, heavenly wisdom, being pure, is "free from 'earthly' principles, pursuits, and goals."—*S.D.A. Bible Commentary,* vol. 7, p. 529.

**Then peaceable.** Heavenly wisdom is not contentious, but conciliatory. It settles quarrels, rather than starting them. See Matthew 5:9. However, it will not accept "peace at any price."

**Gentle.** The Greek word here translated "gentle" is almost untranslatable. The difficulty is indicated by the various renderings. The New English Bible, New International Version, and the Jerusalem Bible have "considerate." Berkeley, Knox, and Weymouth translate, "courteous." C. K. Williams has "without prejudice," and the New American Bible reads, "lenient." The thought may be conveyed by the idea of the "spirit" of the law which tempers the "letter."

**And easy to be entreated.** ("open to reason," RSV) that is unprejudiced, willing to yield to reason. The British poet, Matthew Arnold, coined a happy term which beautifully expresses the idea: "sweet reasonableness."

**Full of mercy.** Having compassion toward those in distress; sympathy and forebearance at the weakness and failures of others. This virtue, as all others, is an attribute of God communicated to the Christian.

**Good fruits.** Practical actions toward people in need, calculated to benefit.

**Without partiality ("without uncertainty," RSV).** The Greek term might be translated unfickle (see chapter 1:6), unambigious, undivided, especially in allegiance to God.

**And without hypocrisy.** The Greek word comes from the stage and has to do with an actor, one who plays a part. Hypocrisy is pretending to be what one is not. A hypocrite is one who deceives in order that others may think him to be what he is not, hoping that he will receive praise for qualities he does not possess.

"The greatest insult we can inflict upon Him [Christ], is to pretend to be His disciples while manifesting the spirit of Satan in our words, our dispositions and our actions."—"Ellen G. White Comments," *S.D.A. Bible Commentary,* vol. 3, p. 1160.

**18. And the fruit (RSV: "harvest") of righteousness is**

**sown in peace of them that make peace.** The harvest that is eventually reaped from righteousness is sown in a spirit of peace by people who are peacemakers. The righteousness that James speaks of is imparted rather than imputed, and imparted righteousness results in the fruits of the Spirit: "love, joy, peace, patience, kindness, goodness, faithfulness, gentleness, self-control." Galatians 5:22, 23, RSV.

1. R. V. G. Tasker, *The General Epistle of James,* Tyndale New Testament Commentaries (Grand Rapids, Mich.: Wm. B. Eerdmans Publishing Co., 1980), p. 77.

2. Richard S. Taylor, ed., *Beacon Dictionary of Theology* (Kansas City: Beacon Hill Press of Kansas City, 1983), p. 434.

3. Carl F. H. Henry, *Christian Personal Ethics* (Grand Rapids, Mich.: Wm. B. Eerdmans Publishing Co., 1957), p. 480.

# CHAPTER 8

# The World and the Will

## James 4:1-12

James introduces this chapter with a question that grows naturally from what he has discussed previously. He has been writing about the evils of the tongue and of some of its evil fruits: bitterness, jealousy, and selfish ambition. This naturally leads to wars and fighting—wider areas of the human problem that rise from those sinful qualities.

**1. From whence come wars and fighting among you?** According to A. T. Robinson, wars refers to "the chronic state or campaign," while fightings means "the separate conflicts or battles in the war."[1]

Does James mean literal or figurative "wars and fightings"? The term "among you" indicates that he has in mind situations among his readers. And the statement "ye kill" in verse 2 seems clearly to indicate literal violence. It is difficult to imagine that he is indicting his Christian readers for literally battling each other and taking life. A charitable solution would be to say that James is thinking of the general human situation and so makes a rather sweeping statement, realizing that some of his readers may also share this spirit and manifest it at times.

It is easy for us to project our thinking back to those early days of the church and fail to connect conditions then with conditions now. But do we not find brother striving with brother today? Do we not see controversies in our churches? Are there not still campaigns waged between various factions? And do not these still create "dissensions, unhappy differences, and petty trials [that] dishonor our Redeemer"?—*Testimonies,* vol. 4, p. 19.

**Come they not hence, even of your lusts that war in your members?** The evils that plague humanity—pride, envy, slander, strife, murder, self-indulgence, covetousness, adultery—have their rise in what James calls "lusts" ("passions," RSV)

The Greek word translated "lust" here is not the same word translated lust in James 1:14, 15. In chapter 4:1 the secular Greek word means "pleasure" or "enjoyment" in the good sense. However, the New Testament always uses it as James does, with the bad connotation of sinful pleasures and enjoyments. James means that sinful humanity has many base desires for self-satisfaction and self-interest, the craving for what one does not have. These desires clamor for gratification through the various body members and are at rest only when indulged. Strife arises when other people become impediments to this gratification.

**2. Ye lust, and have not.** The average English reader will not recognize that the word *lust* in this verse does not come from the same Greek word as does the word *lust* in verse 1. In this verse the Greek word is the same as in James 1:14, 15. Perhaps we can explain the difference this way: In verse 1 the emphasis is on pleasure itself while in verse 2 the stress is on the driving urge to *satisfy* that pleasure. A person in that condition "is not," in the words of D. Martyn Lloyd-Jones, "so much interested in whether a thing is right or not, he is interested in the fact that he wants it, that he likes it, that he must have it."[2]

Commenting on such a situation, the *Dictionary of New Testament Theology* observes that when a person becomes "a slave of their [sinful desires] allurements and temptations his 'heart,' i.e., the centre of his whole personality (Romans 1:24) comes under their control. When this happens all the decisions of the will, and even the best and highest impulses and powers of a man are determined by these desires."[3]

**Ye fight and war, and yet ye have not, because ye ask not.** The effort of professed Christians to satisfy their evil passions and selfish desires inevitably puts them at sword's points with each other, yet does not give them what they want. The reason is that their desires are wrong, their perspective is wrong, their approach is wrong—their life is wrong. They must turn to God, give their sinful desires over to Him, allow Him to purge their passions and change their hearts. They will then pray according to His will, not their own. "This is the confidence which we have in him, that if we ask anything according to his will he hears us." 1 John 5:14, RSV.

**3. Ye ask, and receive not, because ye ask amiss, that ye may consume it upon your lusts.** Could a Christian actually ask God to answer a prayer for the satisfaction of his own wrong desires? The idea sounds incredible. But I recall a particular incident in which I prayed that God would allow me to do something—actually a rather small thing—I wanted very much to do. I wrestled with God, but received no hint that I had His approval. But, like Balaam, I went ahead and did it anyway, even though my conscience bothered me. And I actually prayed while doing it that God would overlook my trespass! It may be helpful to some readers for me to add that the thing I fancied would be so gratifying proved to be but dust and ashes.

**4. Ye adulterers and adulteresses.** Realizing the dismal, self-inflicted spiritual condition of the professed Christians to whom he is writing, James bursts out with reproof.

Only the word *adulteresses* is used in the Greek. The word *adulterers* is supplied, leading us to believe that James is thinking in spiritual rather than literal terms. Paul uses the figure of Christ as a bridegroom and the church as His bride in 2 Corinthians 11:2. The figure of God's people as a woman committing adultery is common in the Old Testament. (See Exodus 34:15; Leviticus 17:7; Deuteronomy 31:16; Isaiah 1:21; Jeremiah 2:20; Ezekiel 16:15.)

**Know ye not that the friendship of the world is enmity with God?** What is meant by "the world," and what is friendship with it? To James, the world is anything around us—material, intellectual, social, and so on—that provides a stimulus for sinful desires. One preacher eloquently described the world thus: "The world is human nature, sacrificing the spiritual to the material, the future to the present, the unseen and eternal to that which touches the senses and which perishes with time. The world is a mighty flood of thoughts, feelings, principles of action, conventional prejudices, dislikes, attachments, which have been gathering around human life for ages, impregnating it, impelling it, moulding it, degrading it. . . . The world at different times wears different forms. Sometimes it is a solid compact mass, an organization of pronounced ungodliness. Sometimes it is a subtle, thin, hardly suspected influence, a power altogether airy and impalpable, which yet does most powerfully penetrate, inform, and shape human life."[4]

"These roads [leading from the strait and the wide gates] are distinct, separate, extending in opposite directions. One leads to eternal death, the other to eternal life. One is broad and smooth, the other narrow and rugged. So the parties that travel them are opposite in character, in life, in dress, and in conversation. Those who travel in the narrow way are talking of the happiness they will have at the end of the journey. . . . They do not dress like the company in the broad road, nor talk like them, nor act like them. A pattern has been given them. A Man of sorrows and acquainted with grief opened that road for them and has traveled it Himself. His followers see His footprints and are comforted and cheered.

"In the broad road all are occupied with their persons, their dress, and the pleasures in the way. . . . Every day they approach nearer their destruction. . . . When it is too late they see that they have gained nothing substantial. They have grasped at shadows and lost eternal life."—*That I May Know Him,* p. 303.

What is friendship with the world? It is thinking in ways that conform to the "world." It is sympathy with, and a desire for, the world's lifestyle. Friendship is a deliberate choice. Figuratively, in James' context, it is a woman who goes out and seeks the companionship of a man who is not her husband. Such an attitude is "enmity with God." *Enmity* is a strong word. It describes a barrier between the soul and God. In our text it means opposition to God's will, active hostility toward Him because of a determination to live one's own life.

**5. Do ye think that the scripture saith in vain, The spirit that dwelleth is us lusteth to envy?** This is a difficult text. *The Seventh-day Adventist Bible Commentary* (vol. 7, p. 532) seems to favor the translation, "The Holy Spirit whom He [God] has caused to dwell within us yearns earnestly with jealousy." Agreeing, H. B. Swete interprets the text: "The Spirit of Christ [the Holy Spirit] in us longs after us, but jealously, with a love which resents any counteracting force such as the friendship of the world. . . . His claim upon the allegiance of the human heart is that of one who can brook no rival; there is a righteous jealousy, as there is a righteous wrath, which is worthy of God and indeed is a necessary consequence of the greatness of His love."[5]

Implicit in our text is tempest in the heart. On the one hand are professed Christians following the flesh, catering to sinful desires, going after the world. On the other hand is the Holy Spirit disturbing people, warning them, inviting them, trying to save them from themselves. Inner turmoil is inevitable under these circumstances.

**6. But he giveth more grace.** Here are encouraging words. A person who is convicted of his need invariably finds himself caught up in a spiritual battle. He is trapped by old sins, enticed by wrong pleasures, and discouraged by past failures. He wants to serve God, but self gets in the way. He feels torn and twisted by it all, as though there is no help anywhere and that struggling is no use. Such a person desperately needs this message: "He giveth more grace."

Grace is God's help far beyond what is deserved or can be expected. Grace is God's strong hand extended to help us, no matter how deeply we may have plunged into sin or how determined our rebellion against Him may have been. Grace is God's supplying us with whatever we need to deal with sin—faith, courage, strength, repentance, forgiveness, cleansing. See Romans 5:20.

But God needs something on the sinner's part before He can extend His grace, and James tells us what that is.

**Wherefore he saith, God resisteth the proud, but giveth grace unto the humble.** God resists the proud because they resist Him. Pride resists because it does not want to admit any need of God. It wants to be independent, putting itself in competition with God as Lucifer did.

Carl F. H. Henry calls pride "the font of sin." C. S. Lewis, who characterizes it as "the great sin," says that pride is essentially competitive. "We say that people are proud of being rich, or clever, or good looking, but they are not. They are proud of being richer, or cleverer, or better looking than others. . . . It's the comparison that makes them proud, the pleasure of being above the rest. . . . The proud man, even when he gets more than he can possibly want, will try to get still more just to assert his power. Nearly all those evils in the world which people put down to greed or selfishness are really the result of Pride."[6]

In 1 Timothy 3:6, Paul warns against giving a new convert a church office because he may be "lifted up" ("puffed up," RSV) with pride. The *Tyndall New Testament Commentary* points out that the word translated "lifted up" means literally, "to wrap in smoke."[1] So we may visualize the humorous picture of a proud person going around, his head enveloped in his little personal smoky cloud of conceit so that he can see only his own importance. Other people, and his own needs, are hidden from him.

We have been thinking of the other person. But it is vital that we examine ourselves. Is it possible that I have been enveloped in my own little cloud of pride?

God's grace, which is not appreciated or desired by pride, is needed to expel pride from the heart. But pride holds shut the door. So it's a bit like a doorkeeper being required to open the door so that he himself might be booted out. This poses a difficult question, the answer to which we will find in verse 7.

**7. Submit yourselves therefore to God.** Pride may be the doorkeeper of the heart, but it does not hold the key. In this text James gets to the keeper of the keys and, in the process, reveals the master key to every door of the human heart. Pride, anger, lust, resentment, covetousness, strife, jealousy—neither a single sin nor the whole host of sins can hold the door closed when the keeper of the key decides to insert it in the lock and swing open the door. That keeper is the will.

Ellen White discusses the subject using another figure: "In surrendering the will, the root of the matter is reached. When the will is surrendered, the streams that flow from the fountain will not be bitter, but will be pure as crystal. The flowers and fruit of the Christian life will bloom and ripen to perfection."— *Signs of the Times,* October 29, 1894. "Everything depends on the right action of the will." (*Steps to Christ,* p. 47), but never on the exercise of the will on its own. "God does not design that our will should be destroyed, for it is only through its exercise that we can accomplish what He would have us do. Our will is to be yielded to Him, that we may receive it again, purified and refined, and so linked in sympathy with the Divine that He can pour through the tides of His love."—*Mount of Blessing,* p. 62.

When we surrender our will to God He accepts, purifies, and strengthens it with His own divine energy and returns it to us. Now our wills harmonize with His, our thoughts are in line with His, our desires reflect His. Now we are ready to deal with sin and Satan because we stand in the strength of another— even Christ.

**Resist the devil, and he will flee from you.** Evil desires, residing in the "flesh" and urged upon us by Satan, may be strong. But God is infinitely stronger and gives His strength to every person who truly submits to Him. Confronted by a resolute will that is fortified by the Spirit's power, Satan recognizes that he can do nothing. He sees a liberating power working in the individual, making it possible for him to do God's will.

"The tempter has no power to control the will or force the soul to sin. He may distress, but he cannot contaminate. He can cause agony, but not defilement. The fact that Christ has conquered should inspire his followers with courage to fight manfully the battle against sin and Satan."—*Review and Herald,* December 17, 1908.

**8. Draw nigh to God, and he will draw nigh to you.** The Greek suggests that we are not to approach Him hesitantly, a step or two, but to stand fully in His presence. We are to "come boldly unto the throne of grace." Hebrews 4:16. Boldly—but not presumptuously or self-confidently. We are to draw near to God through Christ (see Ephesians 2:13) in childlike trust, acknowledging our sinfulness and our weakness, depending on His mercy and His grace.

**Cleanse your hands, ye sinners; and purify your hearts, ye double minded.** In the Old Testament cleansing the hands symbolized the ritual removal of guilt. See Deuteronomy 21:4-7. But God requires much more than ritual cleansing. He wants moral washing, inward purity. See Isaiah 1:15-17. So we may take the words "cleanse your hands" to mean, Let your actions, your lifestyle, reflect the Christianity you profess. But such actions are acceptable to God only when they spring from a purified heart that, through Christ, is made blameless.

James writes as though the purifying is to be done by the sinner. It is, of course, a joint work between the sinner and the Holy Spirit. The strength comes from God; the use of that strength is up to us. We accept divine power and cooperate with the Spirit in expelling sin from our lives.

The term "double minded" is discussed in connection with chapter 1:18.

**9. Be afflicted, and mourn, and weep.** So far James has discussed a number of sin problems, including boasting, uncontrolled tongues, envy, hypocrisy, wars and fightings, lust, selfishness, and worldliness. Now he calls for a change of attitude that means repentance. The genuinely repentant sinner is miserable. See Romans 7:24; Revelation 3:17. But only the Holy Spirit can bring us to this frame of mind, for repentance is a work of God. See Romans 2:4.

**Let your laughter be turned to mourning, and your joy to heaviness.** For the person who insists on having his own way conscience's voice of warning is often covered by merriment and cheap worldly pleasure. Satan is extremely pleased when professed Christians laugh when they should be praying and tell jokes when they should be talking about Jesus.

A. W. Tozer makes a sobering point in this connection: "Let us remember that however jolly we Christians may become, the devil is not fooling. He is cold-faced and serious, and we will find at last that he is playing for keeps. If we who claim to be followers of the Lamb will not take things seriously, Satan will, and he is wise enough to use our levity to destroy us."[8]

Christianity is a joyful religion to those who truly understand it, and God does not mean that we should give that up. "In thy presence is fulness of joy; at thy right hand there are pleasures for evermore." Psalm 16:11; see Job 8:20, 21.

Repentance has four stages:

1. Seeing of oneself from God's point of view.
2. A feeling of revulsion over the ugliness of our sins.
3. Deep, sincere sorrow for sin.
4. Turning away from sin and assuming God's attitude toward it.

"Godly grief produces a repentance that leads to salvation and brings no regret." 2 Corinthians 7:10, RSV.

**Humble yourselves in the sight of the Lord.** As pride is the source of sin so humility is the source of godliness. Thomas Moore wrote,

> Humility, that low, sweet root,
> From which all heavenly virtues shoot.

The Latin root of the word humility means soil or earth. However, the truly humble person is not one who grovels in the dirt. Humility means being down to earth without crawling in it. Christian humility should be accompanied by a sense of our infinite worth to God. Humility that is not seasoned with the salt of heaven is simply a human quality, mixed with human contaminants that will devalue it.

"Those who have had the deepest experience in the things of God, are the farthest removed from pride or self-exaltation. They have the humblest thoughts of self, and the most exalted conceptions of the glory and excellence of Christ. They feel that the lowest place in his service is too honorable for them."— *Review and Herald,* November 18, 1909.

**And he shall lift you up.** This does not mean that God will honor the humble one before the church or the world. God does not promise to give high position or to bring wide acclaim. When we repent, He exalts us to be sons and daughters of God. He gives us a confidence that is not of self but of Himself, so that we may hold up our heads and look every man in the eye.

**11. Speak not evil one of another, brethren.** The Jews used to say that the tongue of the slanderer slew three people: the speaker, the one spoken to, and the one spoken of.

In this exhortation the word *brethren* becomes a rebuke. Brothers and sisters are supposed to love each other, and love does not undermine or destroy. Rather, it reinforces and builds up, especially another brother or sister. But criticism and harsh judgment are nearly always an effort to build up one's own self. They are another proud method to appear better than another, to compare oneself with another so as to appear superior.

"The heart in which love rules will not be filled with passion or revenge, by injuries which pride and self-love would deem unbearable. Love is unsuspecting, ever placing the most favorable construction upon the motives and acts of others. Love will never needlessly expose the faults of others. It does not listen eagerly to unfavorable reports, but rather seeks to bring to mind some good qualities of the one defamed."—*Testimonies*, vol. 5, pp. 168, 169.

**He that speaketh evil of his brother, and judgeth his brother, speaketh evil of the law, and judgeth the law: but if thou judge the law, thou art not a doer of the law, but a judge.** A word is needed here about the Bible's use of the word *judging*. We must differentiate between judging as evaluation and judging as condemnation. Romans 2:1 is often quoted as proof that judgment of any kind is wrong: "Thou art inexcusable, O man, whosoever thou art that judgest." But Paul does not have in mind the very appropriate matter of evaluating people's honesty, sincerity, and general worth. That kind of judgment is important in every area of living. Without it, life would be chaotic. What Paul condemns is judgment that tears down, judgment that is uncharitable, rash, and harsh.

In what way could one who speaks evil against another be said to judge the law? Leviticus 19:15-18 provides one answer. That passage warns against hating "your brother in your heart" (RSV) and against bearing grudges. It concludes with that precept which Christ held up and quoted as the basis of human relationships: "Thou shalt love thy neighbour as thyself." Matthew 22:39. When we assume the judgment seat we elevate ourselves to the role of judge. We put ourselves above the law as though we were qualified to say what or who is right or wrong.

He who treats another in the ways referred to in the above passage is, by his attitude and words, showing that the law is not so important. In that way he judges the law. He assumes authority, not only toward other persons, but toward the law and its Author.

**12. There is one lawgiver, who is able to save and to destroy.** Foolish human beings sit in judgment on other people and offer their petty verdicts, disregarding God's precepts. Out of their overblown pride and selfishness they present what they choose to call facts and offer judgments based on their own ideas of right and wrong rather than on God's.

**Who art thou that judgest another?** In modern terminology, "Who do you think you are? What qualifies you to be a judge? Do you have the right motives? Is your integrity unquestionable? Do you have control of your tongue? Do you have charity toward the person you are judging? Do you have all the facts, and are they all correct? Most important, do you know his motives?" If the answer is No, then do not try to be a judge.

1. A. T. Robertson, *Word Pictures in the New Testament* (Nashville, Tenn.: Broadman Press, 1933), vol. 6, p. 49.

2. D. Martyn Lloyd-Jones, *God's Way of Reconciliation* (Grand Rapids, Mich.: Baker Book House, 1979), p. 62.

3. Colin Brown, ed., *Dictionary of New Testament Theology* (Grand Rapids, Mich.: Zondervan Publishing House, 1975) vol. 1, p. 457.

4. Alfred Plummer, *The General Epistles of St. James and St. Jude,* The Expositor's Bible (New York: P. C. Armstrong and Son, 1903), p. 230.

5. Henry Barclay Swete, *The Holy Spirit in the New Testament* (Grand Rapids, Mich.: Baker Book House, 1976), pp. 257, 258.

6. C. S. Lewis, *Christian Behaviour* (New York: The Macmillan Co., 1948), pp. 45, 46.

7. *Tyndale New Testament Commentary* (Grand Rapids, Mich.: Wm. B. Eerdman's Publishing Co., 1984), vol. 14, p. 82.

8. A. W. Tozer, *Of God and Men* (Harrisburg, Penn.: Christian Publications, Inc., 1960), p. 81.

# CHAPTER 9

# Materialism and the Judgment

## James 4:13 to 5:6

Reading through the fourth chapter of James casually, one might think that the apostle changed subjects abruptly after verse 12. But Lenski does not think so. "Disregard of God is still the underlying thought; in v. 1-10 God is disregarded in preference to the world, in v. 11, 12 God is disregarded by judging a brother, he is now disregarded and ignored when one is planning business—something that is done constantly to this day."[1]

### Chapter 4:13-17

**13. Go to now, ye that say, To day or to morrow we will go into such a city, and continue there a year, and buy and sell, and get gain.** James does not mean that we should avoid making plans. That is essential to success in any venture. Jesus touched on the importance of planning in Luke 14:28-32. Who, He asks, would be so foolish as to build a tower without first figuring whether he had the funds? And what king would consider confronting an army of 20,000 soldiers with only 10,000, unless he could be reasonably confident of winning?

James condemned the tendency to block God out of our plans because of what we today call materialism. Materialism is "the tendency to be more concerned with material than with spiritual . . . goals or values."[2]

One may give lip service to God, claiming that He is first in his life, while his words and actions testify otherwise. The accumulation of riches is such a strong desire to some people that it

81

drowns out every other value, and even the impressions of the Holy Spirit. Men plan that "to day and to morrow" they will "go into such a city, and continue there a year, . . . and get gain," meanwhile leaving God as a shadowy figure lurking in the background who sometimes moves momentarily into the light of conscience but is soon relegated to the shadows again.

**14. Whereas ye know not what shall be on the morrow.** We cannot be sure of what shall be even an hour from now, to say nothing of the next twelve months.

**For what is your life? It is even a vapour, that appeareth for a little time, and then vanisheth away.** The accumulator of riches may go confidently on his way today, in good health, with old age years in the future. But such an attitude is the essence of folly, as Jesus so plainly showed in His parable of the rich fool. See Luke 12:16-21. Life is finite, and as uncertain as it is finite. Thus, anyone who puts anything but God at the center will, sooner or later, face the results of his folly. And that result will be terrible.

A story, no doubt imaginary, is told which points up the uncertainty of life. A businessman dreamed he had been given a newspaper dated two weeks after the time he received it. Elated, he turned to the stock market page. Now he could get a picture of the market two weeks in advance and make a huge profit. He was folding up the paper, after jubilantly getting all the information he wanted, when his eye fell upon a name in the obituary column. It was his own.

**15. For that ye ought to say, If the Lord will, we shall live, and do this, or that.** There are a number of implications in this text that are easy to miss. It suggests that God has an interest in us and our concerns and has plans for us. It assumes that God is in control of things and is able to work things out according to His will. It assumes that we will seek to know His will. This means prayer, pondering the implications of a situation, searching the heart, and perhaps studying what the Word of God says about the matter involved.

This verse also implies that when we know God's will we will choose to follow it. It may not be easy to surrender our plans for His. Nevertheless, Jesus' prayer, "Not my will but thine be done," must be our expression of surrender too.

**16. But now ye rejoice in your boastings: all such rejoicing is evil.** Self-deceived, feeling that our own abilities, cleverness, and strength will bring material success, it is easy to make insolent and empty claims of security because we think we are in control. Such boasting is reprehensible. And to think that James needed to address such words to church members!

**17. Therefore to him that knoweth to do good, and doeth it not, to him it is sin.** James makes this statement in the specific context of the Christian's need to carry on his business transactions in the light of God's will. However, he states a principle that encompasses all of Christian living. As soon as we know that a particular way is right, it is sin to not do it. "If light come, and that light is set aside or rejected, then comes condemnation and the frown of God; but before the light comes, there is no sin, for there is no light for them to reject."—*Testimonies,* vol. 1, p. 116.

How does one know God's will so that he will know how "to do good"? Two primary ways may be suggested:

1. Revelation. The Bible gives specific principles that lead the Christian in all areas having to do with salvation, and the Holy Spirit will guide him in knowing God's will through the Word.

2. Conscience. The conscience is the moral capacity of the mind by which humans can know right from wrong. It is a channel through which the Holy Spirit speaks to heart and mind to direct the Christian in right ways. Conscience must give way to God's Word and must be educated to align with it. See *Testimonies,* vol. 5, pp. 69, 548.

Conscience is not a precise guide because God does not speak to us through it audibly. It operates more like the Yes or No of the Urim and Thummim. Its purpose is frequently to sensitize us to the simple "ought"; a particular act ought, or ought not, to be done.

Does this mean that so long as an individual "lives up to the light he has" he will be saved? Yes and no. Although this question does not fall within the range of James' discussion, it may be useful for us to touch on it here. Salvation does not depend on a person living up to "the light," but upon a connection with Jesus Christ. "Except a man be born again, he cannot see the kingdom of God." John 3:3. This is the irreducible minimum for salvation. If one who has surrendered to Christ and been regenerated is unaware of God's requirements, there is no sin, for there is no light to reject. Yet without the new birth one may live up to every part of the law of which he is aware and still be lost. A converted person will not be lost because he disobeys God without realizing it.

Our text, by implication, involves the will. Doing what is good means making a decision, which is a function of the will. One must resolve before he can act. The true balance between God's will and man's is seen in the following Spirit of Prophecy quotations.

"Man is to make earnest efforts to overcome that which hinders him from attaining to perfection. But he is wholly dependent upon God for success. Human effort of itself is not sufficient. Without the aid of divine power it avails nothing. God works and man works. Resistance of temptation must come from man, who must draw his power from God."—*The Acts of the Apostles,* p. 482.

"What human power can do divine power is not summoned to do. God does not dispense with man's aid. He strengthens him, co-operating with him as he uses the powers and capabilities given him."—*The Desire of Ages,* p. 535.

"Desires for goodness and true holiness are right so far as they go; but if you stop here, they will avail nothing. Good purposes are right, but will prove of no avail unless resolutely carried out. Many will be lost while hoping and desiring to be Christians; but they made no earnest effort, therefore they will be weighed in the balances and found wanting. The will must be exercised in the right direction."—*Testimonies,* vol. 2, pp. 265, 266.

### Chapter 5:1-6

Materialism is a common theme that unites the last few verses of James 4 and the first few verses of chapter 5. In the first case is described heedlessness toward God in gaining wealth, in the latter, heedlessness toward one's fellow man.

James 5:1-6 is black with judgment. It has an air of unrelieved doom. There is no hint of hope, no call for repentance. There is only a note of despair. Nothing is offered but misery, agony, vindication, and certain retribution. It is apparent, therefore, that the judgment into which James thrusts his wealthy readers is the final judgment when the wicked will reap the fruits of their self-centeredness and be "cast out into outer darkness: there shall be weeping and gnashing of teeth." Matthew 8:12. The day of repentance passed by unrecognized and now it is gone forever.

**Go to now, ye rich men, weep and howl for the miseries that shall come upon you.** "Go to now" is an imperative summons that suggests reproof and condemnation, with echoes of Jesus' "Woe unto you!" See Matthew 23:13-16, 25-27.

James' summons to "weep and howl" is reminiscent of the call by Old Testament prophets for people or nations to mourn in view of some terrible calamity. See Isaiah 13:6; Jeremiah 4:8; Zephaniah 1:11. He has previously noted the materialism of the rich. Now he addresses them directly. Yet we must not infer that James is anti-rich. He is concerned for the flock which the rich "wolves" are ravishing.

But neither James nor the Bible as a whole condemn riches as such. "Means is valuable and to be desired. It is a blessing, a precious treasure, if used prudently, wisely, and not abused."— *Our High Calling,* p. 193. But so often wealth and the advantages it accrues are abused.

**2. Your riches are corrupted, and your garments are motheaten.** Riches here would include crops, and the meaning could be that their owner had stored them so long, instead of sharing them, that they spoiled. Likewise, their fine wardrobe, stored away in chests, may have been consumed by mold and moths, and so were made useless.

**3. Your gold and silver is cankered; and the rust of them shall be a witness against you, and shall eat your flesh as it were fire.** James employs a bold figure to try to drive home to his wealthy readers the peril of avarice. Gold and silver rust, he says, and the rust bites into your flesh like fire. Of course, neither actually happens in nature. But the vivid language must have gripped the imagination of his Oriental readers, who had no trouble understanding figures of speech that sound strange to our Western ears.

**Ye have heaped treasure together for the last days.** The rich accumulate treasure that will condemn them in the judgment. Paul counseled Timothy to exhort the rich to lay "up in store for themselves a good foundation against the time to come [the judgment], that they may lay hold on eternal life." 1 Timothy 6:19. They were to do this by being "rich in good works, ready to distribute, willing to communicate." Verse 18.

**4. Behold, the hire of the labourers who have reaped down your fields, which is of you kept back by fraud, crieth.** The Greek tells us that the harvest is finished. The crops have been gathered in. This suggests that the rich landowners garnered a tidy profit from the new crop, but they callously refused to pay their workers. The rich became richer, the poor poorer. Apparently the withholding of wages was not an uncommon practice in Bible times, for we have a number of references to it in the Old Testament. See Leviticus 19:13; Deuteronomy 24:14, 15; Job 24:10; Proverbs 3:27, 28; Jeremiah 22:13; Malachi 3:5.

Avarice is one of the hungriest passions of the human soul. There have always been people who were dissatisfied with the fair gain that comes through the honest use of brain and muscle. They have a passion to amass more and more, faster and faster. In doing so they sweep aside the God-given instinct for justice and social right, and assume the hard selfishness that can so easily become a part of business. They scheme to get the fruits of other's labors unfairly. Sometimes they do this by raw force, as in the case of King Ahab, who murdered Naboth to get his vineyard. See 1 Kings 21:1-16. More often, they do it by subterfuge. Greedy men, endowed with cunning and lack of principle, use their cleverness and position to take advantage of others who are not so well qualified intellectually, physically, socially, culturally, or racially.

Often, the wealth and position of these men place them above retribution in this life. It is well-known that the powerful commit serious crimes and receive little more than a slap on the wrist, whereas someone without influence, committing a much less serious crime, may receive a long prison term.

Nor are the crimes with which James indicts his rich readers altogether absent from the Christian church. "Because avarice and treachery are seen in the lives of those who have named the name of Christ, because the church retains on her books the names of those who have gained their possessions by injustice, the religion of Christ is held in contempt. Extravagance, over-reaching, extortion, are corrupting the faith of many and destroying their spirituality."—*Prophets and Kings,* p. 651.

**The cries of them which have reaped are entered into the ears of the Lord of sabaoth.** Sabaoth is not the same as Sabbath. Sabaoth is a transliteration both in the Greek and in English, of a common Hebrew word that is usually translated "hosts." The reference is probably to the vast armies of heaven. See Joshua 5:14; 1 Kings 22:19; 2 Chronicles 18:18. Applied to God, the term took on the meaning of Sovereign or Almighty.

The pitiful cry of the wronged and helpless workers is heard by the omnipotent God, who will lead forth His armies to avenge those who, exploited and oppressed by the powers of earth, cannot avenge themselves.

**5. Ye have lived in pleasure on the earth, and been wanton; ye have nourished your hearts, as in a day of slaughter.** The judgments of God do not always wait for the final day. Throughout history, He has sometimes allowed judgments to fall.

We wonder if any of the rich Jews who lived in self-indulgent luxury and who read the words of James were in Jerusalem in A.D. 70 and, in horrible anguish, recalled them. Josephus indicates that the rich, trapped in the city, specially suffered.[3] Caught "between a rock and a hard place," they had no escape. Many of them had been friendly with the Romans, and thus provoked the envy and enmity of the fanatical, murderous Zealots who controlled the city. Thus, whether the rich remained in the city during the seige or tried to escape made no difference. They were equally doomed either way. Every Jew who was known to have had dealings with the Romans was put to death on the pretext that he planned to desert, but in reality that the plundering Zealots might get his possessions. Anyone who appeared half-starved was left alone when he protested that he had nothing. Anyone whose body showed no sign of privation was tortured to force him or her to tell where he had hidden his treasures.

"The visitation of judgments upon Jerusalem is to have another fulfillment, of which that terrible desolation was but a faint shadow."—*The Great Controversy,* p. 36.

The attitude of the persecuted toward his persecutors is described in pathos: "He doth not resist you." Defenseless, having learned the futility of resistance, knowing no recourse but God, he waits in resignation for a time when deliverance will indeed come from God.

**6. Ye have condemned and killed the just; and he doth not resist you.** Says Lenski, "However innocent a man might be, these rich fellows found ways and means to condemn him when they so pleased, be it in their own Jewish courts or before pagan tribunals. This condemnation sometimes resulted in the execution of the innocent. To this limit these unscrupulous rich went."[4]

We may think that James' description of the rich and the oppressed does not fit our world. The average person in the West has workmen's unions and recourses to the law. But such checks and balances do not necessarily guarantee justice. In many parts of the world the poor and the unimportant still have problems, not only getting their cases heard fairly, but sometimes just getting them heard at all.

1. R. C. H. Lenski, *The Interpretation of the Epistle to the Hebrews and the Epistle of James* (Minneapolis: Augsburg Publishing House, 1966), p. 638.

2. *Webster's New World Dictionary,* second college edition.

3. Flavius Josephus, *Wars of the Jews,* book 5, ch. 10, par. 2.

4. Lenski, p. 652.

# CHAPTER 10

# Waiting for the Harvest

## James 5:7-20

Having addressed the rich exploiter, James now turns to the poor exploited. What does one do when he has been cheated of his living and has virtually no recourse? How does one advise such a person? The problem is a difficult one for the adviser as well as the victim. James' immediate answer takes the long view.

**7. Be patient therefore, brethren, unto the coming of the Lord.** The underlying concept of the Greek word translated "patient" is "catch your breath for a long race." Vincent informs us that the term suggests "a long-protracted restraint of the soul from yielding to passion, especially the passion of anger."[1]

This counsel casts some light on the phrase "he does not resist you" in verse 6. It does not tell us that the wronged ones, sheeplike, almost unaware that they are being wronged, are herded about at their oppressor's will. They are keenly aware of the injustice of their situation, but they also know that there is nowhere in the human sphere to turn for redress.

R. V. G. Tasker observes that the Greek term "denotes not so much the brave endurance of afflictions and the refusal to give way before them even under pressure, as the self-restraint which enables the sufferer to refrain from hasty retaliation. The opposite of 'patience' in this sense are wrath and revenge."[2]

**Behold, the husbandman waiteth for the precious fruit**

**of the earth, and hath patience for it, until he receive the early and the latter rain.** The patience that the farmer shows toward his crop is based on his knowledge of nature's operations. He knows that it takes just so long for seeds to grow and mature, that it takes so much rain, so much sun. His patience, then, is geared to the pace of nature. He does not expect a harvest when the normal growing period is only half completed.

Similarly, James admonishes his oppressed readers to wait patiently for the final harvesttime. They cannot know God's timetable for that harvest as the farmer understands nature's timetable. But they can trust that "God's purposes know no haste and no delay."—*The Desire of Ages,* p. 32. They can know that He will not put off the harvest a moment longer than is necessary to bring all things to proper maturity.

**8. Be ye also patient; stablish your hearts: for the coming of the Lord draweth nigh.** Oppression and injustice, scorn, temptation, and want, are your lot, James acknowledges. But "stablish your hearts" ("be . . . stouthearted," NEB; "keep your hopes high," TEV; "keep up your courage," Goodspeed; "fortify your hearts," Berkeley). Set your hearts firmly upon the blessed hope, James says. Don't be shaken or discouraged but "steadfast, unmovable, always abounding in the work of the Lord, foreasmuch as ye know that your labour is not in vain in the Lord." 1 Corinthians 15:58.

**9. Grudge not one against another, brethren, lest ye be condemned: behold, the judge standeth at the door.** "Grudge," better, complain, murmur, grumble, was the meaning of *grudge* when the King James Version was published. The caution may refer to a complaining under the breath. It suggests a barely suppressed condemnation or judgment, simmering in the heart which could at times break out in more open expression. The words "one against another" hint at the complaining as a sort of mutual recrimination.

The attitude behind the murmuring is wrong and, by the grace of God, must be resisted and overcome for it tends not only to tension and trouble between brethren but indicates a rancor in the heart which destroys spirituality and happiness. Anyone who allows an attitude of condemnatory judgment to persist merits the final condemnation of the Great Judge. Paul warned of the ultimate results of murmuring. "Neither murmur ye," he wrote to the Corinthian Christians, "as some of them [the Israelites] also murmured, and were destroyed of the destroyer." 1 Corinthians 10:10.

**10. Take, my brethren, the prophets, who have spoken in the name of the Lord, for an example of suffering affliction, and of patience.** Murmuring and complaining show a lack of patience. James cites the prophets, many of whom underwent much more persecution than his readers were experiencing. Actually, in most cases, little is recorded of the prophets' sufferings though Stephen implied that virtually all of them were persecuted. See Acts 7:52; see also Hebrews 11:36-38. All of those men were "subject to like passions as we are." James 5:17. Some of them may have been naturally impatient. See Ezekiel 3:14; Habakkuk 1:1-13. But by the Spirit they were able to maintain a godly longsuffering that kept them from retaliation, from breaking out in action and word, enabling them to wait patiently for God to work things out in His time and way.

The observation that the prophets spoke in the Lord's name suggests that either they suffered persecution as a result of their speaking or in spite of it. Their role as prophets of God did not protect them from persecution.

**11. Behold, we count them happy which endure. Ye have heard of the patience of Job.** The root of our word *happy* is the old English word, *hap,* meaning "chance," "fortune." And what we think of as happiness generally depends on whether events and circumstances "happen" in our favor. But the context of happiness in our text is not pleasant circumstances or events. Quite the opposite. For, while James submits Job as an example of a happy man, Job's circumstances were far from happy, as we know. James may be suggesting, then, that the knowledge that one has been steadfast in his allegiance to God brings a sense of blessing in spite of circumstances. And the next phrase may suggest yet another reason for happiness in adversity.

**And have seen the end ["purpose," RSV] of the Lord; that**

**the Lord is very pitiful, and of tender mercy.** Linked with the foregoing thought, this may be understood to mean that Job experienced happiness after his severe test, when he understood God's purpose in permitting it, and when "the Lord blessed the latter end of Job more than his beginning." Job 42:12.

**12. But above all things, my brethren, swear not, neither by heaven, neither by the earth, neither by any other oath: but let your yea be yea; and your nay, nay; lest ye fall into condemnation.** Today's English Version is helpful in understanding this text: "Above all, my brothers, do not use an oath when you make a promise." Apparently the people used oaths to secure the most trivial statements. This devalued all such oaths, making them virtually worthless, especially when their word proved false. That is why James advised not to use oaths at all. If your word is not good, the proliferation of oaths will not make it so.

Cursing expletives are also included. Some common English exclamations that are used by some Christians are actually "pious oaths." For example, *gee* is a contraction of the word *Jesus,* and *gosh* and *golly* are variations on God's name.

There were certain situations in which oaths properly were taken during Bible times. See Deuteronomy 10:20; Isaiah 65:16; Jeremiah 4:2; 12:16; 2 Corinthians 1:23; Galatians 1:20.

**13. Is any among you afflicted? let him pray.** Suffering comes in many forms, and often there is little that fellow humans can do to ease it. Only God can relieve the distress or give grace to endure. Sometimes there is little we can do but pray. But the prayer of faith finds an answer in comfort, strength, and help.

**Is any merry? let him sing psalms.** The Revised Standard Version has "cheerful," which is perhaps better than "merry." Today merriment suggests hilariousness, with its facetious spirit that is inappropriate for Christians. See on chapter 4:9. The singing of psalms does not suggest hilarity. Christian cheerfulness soars higher and rings clearer than merriment, because it echoes from a soul that is the dwelling place of Christ's Spirit.

**14. Is any sick among you? let him call for the elders of**

**the church; and let them pray over him, anointing him with oil in the name of the Lord.** James did not intend to write the last word on how sickness is to be dealt with. For example, he did not mean that a physician is never to be called. Jesus did not belittle physicians. See Matthew 9:12; Luke 4:23. Paul's companion, Luke, was a well-regarded physician. See Colossians 4:14. Praying for the sick is a serious act which must be undertaken only after much soul-searching.

**15. And the prayer of faith shall save the sick, and the Lord will raise him up.** Again, James seems to assume certain things. He does not say that the prayer must be offered in submission to God who will do the best thing. When prayers are offered in faith from hearts pure before God, we are assured that "recoveries will follow"—*Counsels on Health,* p. 210. Yet we must not assume that recovery will always follow, nor lose faith when it does not.

**And if he have committed sins, they shall be forgiven him.** Implicit in these words is the idea that the sick individual will repent unreservedly of his sins. The "if" does not mean he has not sinned. "All have sinned." Romans 3:23. Rather, it suggests that if his illness was occasioned by particular sins, his healing will show they are forgiven.

**16. Confess your faults one to another, and pray one for another, that ye may be healed.** "All are liable to err, therefore the Word of God tells us plainly how to correct and heal the mistakes. . . . Whatever the character of your sin, confess it. If it is against God only, confess only to Him. If you have wronged or offended others, confess also to them, and the blessing of the Lord will rest upon you. In this way you die to self, and Christ is formed within."—*That I May Know Him,* p. 239.

"Be sure that the confession fully covers the influence of the wrong committed, that no duty to God, to your neighbor, or to the church is left undone, and then you may lay hold of Christ with confidence, expecting His blessing."—*Testimonies,* vol. 5, p. 646.

**The effectual fervent prayer of a righteous man availeth much.** Most versions agree that the thrust of this phrase is, The prayer of a righteous man is powerful and effective. A righteous person is one who, having committed his life to God, seeks in heart, mind, and life to conform fully to His requirements. The righteous man not only prays, he also obeys. Because he is fully committed, he has no accusing conscience to weaken his petition, no shame to temper his faith. God is pleased to honor the prayer of such a person. A virtuous life erects no barriers that make it difficult for God to work.

**17. Elias was a man subject to like passions as we are.** "Like passions" is misleading. James means that Elijah was as human as we are, with the same limitations we have. But his faith enabled him to rise above human doubts, to sweep aside impossibilities, placing total confidence in what God can do.

**19. Brethren, if any of you do err from the truth, and one convert him.** Even the most committed Christian may wander from the truth. When the spiritual eye is taken off Jesus, it may very soon be caught by one of Satan's intriguing subtleties. Then, unless there is an immediate turning back to Jesus, the mind is led by guileful ways, spiritual perception is paralyzed, and error accepted. See comment on James 1:13-15. Thus, the path from truth is also the path from Christ. We must always lead people to truth in the Lord Jesus.

**20. Let him know, that he which converteth the sinner from the error of his way, shall save a soul from death.** To save a soul from the error of his way is, with the Spirit's aid, to lead him to repent of and confess his error, which restores him to his relationship with Jesus and thus rescues him from eternal death.

**And shall hide a multitude of sins.** Hide does not mean a "cover up," with the sins still there. It means the sins are forsaken and forgiven. Psalm 32:1 summarizes the thought: "Blessed is he whose transgression is *forgiven,* whose sin is *covered.*" Emphasis supplied.

1. Marvin R. Vincent, *Word Studies in the New Testament* (Grand Rapids, Mich.: Wm. B. Eerdmans Publishing Co., 1976), vol. 1, p. 761.

2. R. V. G. Tasker, *The General Epistle of James,* Tyndale New Testament Commentaries (Grand Rapids, Mich.: Wm. G. Eerdmans Publishing Co., 1980), p. 117.

# CHAPTER 11
# The Halfway Covenant

In Northampton, Massachusetts, a Congregational minister knelt in prayer. He felt deeply burdened for the souls of that little town who, he was convinced, were afflicted with a deadly spiritual disease. That day in 1734 marked the birth of one of the most notable religious revivals that North America has ever known. The conditions that pressed Jonathan Edwards to his knees that Sunday seemed black indeed. Gone was the God-fearing generation that had settled the land. The new generation had forgotten God. Immorality, debauchery, and self-interest ruled. Few worried about the next world. Even those who held the externals of religion had lost its heart. Church rolls were shriveling. Conditions had become so bad that in 1662 the leading ministers of the Massachusetts colony did something they thought would help, but which actually made things worse. They adopted what was called the Halfway Covenant. People who could make no profession of regeneration still could get their children baptized, so long as they assented to the doctrine of faith and were not "scandalous in life." When their children grew up, if *they* could not testify to conversion, they were denied only one privilege. They could not partake of the Lord's Supper.

These halfway members soon outstripped the members in full communion. Halfway membership was socially acceptable. Why bother going all the way? Eventually the Lord's Supper dropped away. It was not long before halfway covenanters filtered into the ministry itself!

A godly remnant soon realized that the Halfway Covenant was a terrible mistake. Something cataclysmic must happen to prevent the flickering flame of vital Christianity from being snuffed out. As He so often does, God chose a man to unlatch the windows of these darkened churches to let in the light. That man was Jonathan Edwards.

In 1734 he began a series of sermons on justification by faith alone. He swept away the hopes of heaven upon which so many of his congregation had rested. Their morality, their membership in the church through the Halfway Covenant, their partaking of the Lord's Supper—all this availed nothing, Edwards told them, nor did he give a mere theological discourse. He relentlessly called the roll of the town sins: irreverence in God's house, disregard of the Sabbath, neglect of family prayer, disobedience to parents, quarreling, greediness, sensuality, hatred of one's neighbor. Every secret sin was held up for all to see.

The Holy Spirit used the sharp edges of these sermons to cut deep. People couldn't sleep on Sunday nights. The next day they could talk of nothing but the amazing upheaval in the pulpit.

The first conversions came in December—five or six "savingly converted," among them a young woman notorious as a "company keeper." The news of her conversion seemed to be like a flash of lightning upon the hearts of the young people, and upon many others.

"Presently upon this," Edwards wrote in his *Narrative of Surprising Conversions,* "a great and earnest concern about the great things of religion and the eternal world became universal in all parts of town, and among persons of all degrees and all ages; the noise among the dry bones waxed louder and louder; all other talk but about spiritual and eternal things were soon thrown by."

The revival spilled over into other towns, and before long 100 communities were affected.[1]

That movement, known as the Great Awakening, became one of the most outstanding revivals in American history, revitalizing the religious experience of tens of thousands of people on the North American continent.

Obviously there are parallels in the condition of those who had taken the Halfway Covenant in Jonathan Edwards' time to the spiritual condition of the Jews in the time of Malachi. They also had taken a halfway covenant, although they did not call it that. The book of Nehemiah describes what most likely was the last great reformation among the Jews. With characteristic zeal, Nehemiah set about to purify the church of his day. His reform was a dramatic one. In fact, we are told that the people of Judah brought "the tithe of the grain, wine, and oil into the storehouses." Nehemiah 13:12, RSV. It is interesting that faithfulness in tithing accompanied reform. But, from the tone of the book of Malachi, it is evident that selfishness again crept into the hearts of priests and people alike. They began to neglect the temple services and their religious responsibilities. As a result, they sank to a new low in their relationship with God.

Although Malachi's messages present a strong condemnation of the lukewarm attitude that characterized the Jews in the period before the Messiah came, the last five verses of the last chapter conclude not only Malachi's prophecy but the entire Old Testament with a promise of the glorious final revival and reformation that is to precede the second coming of Christ. To those of us eagerly anticipating and praying for revival and reformation in the church today, there can be no question about the significance of Malachi to the Laodicean church.

After the brief introduction in the first verse of the book, most of the remainder is taken up with God's warnings on one hand and the people's self-righteous denials on the other. They seemed to ignore God's warnings because they felt that they did not need them. Between chapters 1:1 and 3:15 we discover eight sets of warnings followed by the people's denials. In the King James Version, six of the eight responses coming from the indifferent people begin with the word *wherein*.

These denials begin in chapter 1 with Israel, the people God had delivered from Egypt and from Babylon, impatiently denying God's affirmations of love for them. "Wherein hast thou loved us?" they rudely respond, ignoring all that God has done for Israel since He called Abram out of Ur.

The selfishness of the priests particularly stands out in verse 7. God charges these religious leaders with offering blind, lame, and sick animals for sacrifice. Rather indignantly, God points out that they should not be so rude as to present to their governor the shabby specimens that they seemed to think God would be pleased to accept. Their sense of sacredness had been dimmed by a stronger sense of selfishness. They wanted to keep the best for themselves and let God have what they did not think was of value to them. They would not even perform the simplest of services in the temple without expecting some remuneration for themselves. See chapter 1:10. The shackles of self had replaced their spirit of service. Their experience is too often duplicated today.

Tragically, many so-called Christians have been trapped in the quest for self at a time when more than 3.5 billion people have never been confronted with the claims of the gospel. Popular best sellers admonish us to assert ourselves and put others down before they get the upper hand. We are not to stand for being "pushed around," they insist; and, above all, we should never let anyone make us feel guilty about our new assertive behavior.

The slogans that sell these days make generous use of such terms as *self-enhancement, self-affirmation, self-actualization, self-discovery, self-acceptance, self-enrichment,* self, self, self, self. We cannot help but wonder whatever happened to the virtues of self-denial, self-sacrifice, self-distrust, self-discipline, self-forgetfulness, and self-control.

As a consequence of all this, it seems almost alien in this existential age to heed Christ's admonition to deny ourselves and take up our cross and follow Him. Yet the shackles of self serve only to perpetuate our slavery to sin. Ellen White wrote, "Self-serving has *no place* in his [the Christian's] life."—*Testimonies,* vol. 7, p. 10, emphasis supplied. The major reason given for this is that self-serving gets in the way of our service for others. In the same reference we find this additional challenge: "The same intensity of desire to save sinners that marked the life of the Saviour marks the life of His true follower. The Christian has no desire to live for self. He delights to consecrate all that he has and is to the Master's service. He is moved by an inexpressible desire to win souls for Christ. Those who have nothing of this desire might better be concerned for their own salvation. Let them pray for the spirit of service."—*Ibid.*

Everything in the world about us seems to communicate the spirit of materialism rather than the spirit of service. It is difficult not to be caught up in this materialistic rat race. Counteracting this prevailing spirit, however, is our deep conviction that the coming of Christ is nearer than we think. We have no time to serve self when there are so many about us who have never been confronted with the claims of the gospel. If we see that self is getting in the way of our service for Christ, we must pray as never before for the spirit of service.

### "What a Weariness!"

In spite of God's concern and His desire to awaken priests and people to the folly of their half-hearted service, they responded with a reply that staggers us with their lack of perception. "What a weariness this is" (verse 13, RSV), we hear them sigh.

Next God sharply points out their infidelity in their relationships with Him and with one another. They have engaged in both spiritual and literal adultery.

At last God tells those who consider His service a weariness that they have "wearied" Him (Malachi 2:17) with their words. Even this desperate condemnation makes no impression on them. In injured tones, they reply, "Wherein have we wearied him?" In other words, "Why? What have we done? What is the matter with You?"

God answers in essence: "You do not even know the difference between evil and good. You do not seem to realize that I am a God of justice and judgment." Their response brings vividly to mind many who echo their spiritual dullness today: "Where is the God of judgment?" Verse 17. We should not be deceived by such specious arguments. God is not mocked. What a person is, he is. The righteous are righteous, and the wicked are wicked. Of course, that can change. God *can* make the wicked righteous; they do not just become sugarcoated sinners. Righteousness is not some sort of God-proof cloak that we put on the outside to keep God from seeing the rottenness underneath. Neither is it a judgment-proof vest that we wear in a vain attempt to escape damage from the talent-size hailstones of the seventh plague. When God makes us righteous, we are righteous through and through.

When you stick a long, sharp needle into a righteous person, wickedness does not ooze out. But what about the thief on the cross? Was he just covered over with an aluminum-foil wrapping of apparent righteousness while his inside remained as rotten as before? No. He was converted. The entire direction of his life changed. He had been plunging down the path to hell and destruction, but the direction of his life changed instantly, and he headed for the stars—toward heaven. A real change took place in that instant of conversion, not just a cosmetic one. What he once hated he now loved. What he once loved he now hated. He was just as converted on the cross as if he had been a free, loving, witnessing Christian for forty years.

Righteousness gets to the core of our being and does something drastic to us. Right *being* is evidenced in right *doing*. This is not our doing. But that which seemed impossible (and *is* impossible except for the miracle of a changed heart) takes place when we fully surrender and let Christ take over our lives.

God never makes evil appear good. He can remake evil people, but to do so He must take the evil out of them, not just cover it up. The book of Romans makes it clear that the new birth involves a complete change in the entire life—a change in:

1. Direction—Romans 6:1-4
2. Perspective—Romans 8:5
3. Dominion—Romans 6:14
4. Masters—Romans 6:16, 22
5. Expected rewards—Romans 6:23
6. Concerns—Romans 8:5, 6
7. Nature—Romans 8:9, 10
8. Behavior—Romans 8:13
9. Relationships—Romans 8:14-17.

When God changes us, he changes all that we are and all with which we are concerned.

**A "Royal Priesthood"**

Malachi 2:5-9 develops a concept that has great significance for those in the last days who are called to "keep the commandments of God, and the faith of Jesus." Revelation 14:12. Because of the faithfulness of the tribe of Levi when the rest of the nation worshiped the golden calf (see Exodus 32:26-28), God chose the Levites for His special service as priests.

Numbers 25:12, 13 tells how a "covenant of peace" later was made with Phinehas. Malachi 2:5 calls this covenant one of "life and peace." God's part in this arrangement was to give life and peace to those faithful to Him. The priests' part was to reverence and obey God. They also were given the responsibility of instructing the people in the law or torah. As the religious leaders of the nation, their commission was to teach, not only by precept but also by example. Because the priests of Malachi's day had failed to live up to their expected part in the covenant of peace, the people could not help but treat them with contempt and also look down upon the religion the priests were supposed to uphold. See Malachi 2:9.

Today God wants to make this same covenant of life and peace with His people who are called to be "a chosen generation, a royal priesthood." 1 Peter 2:9. But we have a responsibility. "The Lord requires of all who profess to be His people, far more than they can give Him. He expects believers in Christ Jesus to reveal to the world, in word and deed, the Christianity that was exemplified in the life and character of the Redeemer. If the Word of God is enshrined in their hearts, they will give a practical demonstration of the power and purity of the gospel."—"Ellen G. White Comments," *S.D.A. Bible Commentary,* vol. 4, p. 1181.

By precept and example God's people, His royal priesthood, today are to uphold the law of God before a world that largely has turned against the Ten Commandments.

**Reborn Free**

Each one of God's laws is good, not evil. The apostle Paul testifies that "the law is holy, and the commandment holy, and just, and good." Romans 7:12. But even in a large segment of today's Christian world, God's laws have been given a bad press. The writings of Paul himself have been twisted out of context to make him say that God's laws are unnecessary as well as unnecessarily confining to people's freedom—just the opposite of what he intended to say. Paul's comments about law in Romans and Galatians must be understood in the context of his controversy with the Judaizers. He made the point that the good laws God had given concerning ceremonies, ordinances, and temple ritual pointed to Christ's death. Because His death was now an accomplished fact, they no longer had the significance or value they once had.

Paul always upheld God's laws. He never condemned them. What he did condemn was the legalism that had become associated with the practice of those laws. Although many misunderstand this point, there is quite a difference between condemning legalism and condemning God's laws. The Pharisees of Jesus' day have had a bad press in today's Christian world too. If ever there was a people trying hard to be good, it was the Pharisees. Unfortunately, they thought that their efforts to keep the law would earn their salvation. They added innumerable laws and interpretations to the few laws that God had given. They went to great lengths to determine every possible variation from the letter of the law, and to fill in perceived breaches, arguing endlessly over minor questions of interpretation and application. But no one can make up enough laws to cover every possible application and situation. With billions of people occupying our globe, the possibility of applications far outraces our capability of developing rules to govern them.

One day on my way to a Japanese language school in Tokyo, I tried to leave through the door of the metro train I was riding, but the crush of people surging in made my exit nearly impossible. Had I not been as tall and large as I was, I do not believe that I could have made it out. The Japanese people, who were so polite in their homes when we visited them, seemed to forget about courtesy and kindness when it came to getting on and off of trains. I asked one of my language teachers why this great difference in behavior on the part of the Japanese. She told me that the Japanese code of extreme politeness and courtesy dated back to the Confucian era, long before there were trains. Therefore behavior on trains was not controlled by their code of politeness.

That is an example of what can happen when mores and behavior are governed by rules. On the other hand, freedom is not to be equated with doing just what we want to do. If it were, society would be in more trouble than it is currently. Following the concept that each man has a right to do his own thing, airline pilots might only show up for work when they felt like it. Druggists and grocers, doctors and policemen could take the same attitude. But this would result in anarchy, not freedom. A society based on this ethic would soon cease to function.

True freedom comes when we place ourselves fully in accord with the Creator's laws that were designed for the full, happy, and peaceful operation of this universe. "The law of love being the foundation of the government of God, the happiness of all intelligent beings depends upon their perfect accord with its great principles of righteousness."—*Patriarchs and Prophets,* p. 34. This is true of the laws of our being as well as of the Ten Commandments. Instead of claiming that we are born free in this world of sin, it might be more accurate to say that we are "reborn free," because only in Christ do we find that true freedom that enables us to live in harmony with the laws of life.

## A Christlike Life Is Accessible

Some, even among Adventists, believe that it is not possible for people today to follow the example of Jesus. But no Adventist who accepts Ellen White as an inspired witness can deny that she takes the plain, unequivocal position that it is possible for us to live as Jesus lived—physically, mentally, socially, and spiritually. The theme that runs as a golden thread through *The Desire of Ages* is that, through the same divine help available to Him, it is possible for us to live a Christlike life. We do not have space to include every reference to this thought found in *The Desire of Ages,* but the following will establish the point. "He [Christ] exercised in His own behalf no power that is not freely offered to us. As man, He met temptation, and overcame in the strength given Him from God. . . . His life testifies that it is possible for us also to obey the law of God."—Page 24. "There was in Him nothing that responded to Satan's sophistry. He did not consent to sin. Not even by a thought did He yield to temptation. So it may be with us."—Page 123. "There is no excuse for sinning. A holy temper, a Christlike life, is accessible to every repenting, believing child of God. . . . As the Son of man was perfect in His life, so His followers are to be perfect in their life."—Page 311. "As Christ lived the law in humanity, so we may do if we will take hold of the Strong for strength."—Page 668. "All who consecrate soul, body, and spirit to God will be constantly receiving a new endowment of physical and mental power. . . . Christ gives them the breath of His own spirit, the life of His own life. . . . Through co-operation with Christ they are complete in Him, and in their human weakness they are enabled to do the deeds of Omnipotence."—Page 827.

With promises such as these we cannot afford to let anyone persuade us that it is impossible to live Christlike lives. The good news is that we *can* follow Christ's example.

Why is following Christ's example of such great importance? Because our mission is to give the world a living representation of our Lord and to demonstrate that people everywhere can live His kind of life. This challenge and this possibility caused Ellen White to call attention to the fact that "if everyone who claims to be a child of God would cherish the spirit of kindness and love, without base thoughts and undue attention, and devote his God-given powers to spreading the truth, in seeking to save souls, what a bright, steady light would shine forth to the world!" She adds: "Let all who profess to be Christians open the door of their hearts to His Spirit and to His grace; then the peace of Christ will so rule in their hearts and be revealed in their characters that there will be no discord, no strife, no emulation, no biting and devouring one another, no seeking for the supremacy. The great and earnest effort will be to live the life of Christ. We are to represent His spirit of mercy and give no occasion for anyone to follow our example in doing evil.

"Jesus was courteous, benevolent. He was obedient to all of His Father's commandments, implicitly and without questioning convenience or any selfish interest. It is enough to us to know that God has spoken; and when we know His will as revealed in His Word, we are to obey."—*This Day With God,* p. 207.

Because God does not ask us to do that which is impossible, He *has* made it possible for us to live Christlike lives. The temptation is to pass such statements off as overly idealistic and impractical. But if we take God at His word we will lift our sights to the thrilling heights that He challenges us to scale, realizing that Christ already has prepared the way for us to reach what we never could on our own. A life like His *can* be ours. Heaven has pledged itself to make it possible. Instead of hanging back in disbelief, let us with grateful hearts accept God's promise and begin, by His grace and power, to live up to the potential that is ours in Christ.

A revival of true godliness among us is our greatest need today. That revival *must* and *will* begin soon. We need to ask ourselves: Why not now? Why not with me? Why not?

1. Adapted by permission from *America's Great Revivals,* published by Bethany House Publishers, Minneapolis, Minnesota 55438, copyrighted by *Sunday Magazine,* Inc.

# CHAPTER 12

# Laodicea: Judging the People

At the conclusion of Malachi 2 we found the people skeptically inquiring, "Where is the God of judgment?" God answers in chapter 3. Verse 1 speaks of two messengers. First, it predicts the coming of the messenger who was to prepare the way of the Lord—John the Baptist. He was to be followed by the "messenger of the covenant"—Jesus. In verses 2 and 3 we find a dual application of Christ's coming. "This prophecy regarding the 'messenger of the covenant' applies not only to the time when Christ came to His Temple during His first advent . . . , but also to the events connected with the close of earth's history and the second advent."—*S.D.A. Bible Commentary*, vol. 4, p. 1130. In a special way the terms "refiner's fire" and "fullers' soap" used in verse 2, point forward to the beginning of the pre-advent, investigative judgment when Christ began His second-apartment ministry in 1844.

Some Adventists today question why there must be an investigative judgment. Is it for God's benefit? No, they answer. God already knows who will be saved and who will be lost. Is it for our benefit then? No, they answer, because there is a review designed for our benefit during the millennium. The implication left is that there is no need for an investigative judgment. But such a superficial conclusion finds its basis on grounds other than what actually is taking place during the investigative judgment now going on in heaven.

First of all, the investigation *is* for God's benefit. Of course, it does not make up His mind as to who is going to be saved. He

106

knows that already. The investigative judgment finds its purpose in the vindication of the character of God by answering the questions Satan has raised concerning the fairness of God's laws and His dealings with created beings. It demonstrates clearly that God will not destroy a rebellious or sinful being until that being has been given every opportunity to be reconciled with God. Before He excludes anyone from coming up in the first resurrection, God must demonstrate that He gave every individual who ever lived a fair chance. He must also demonstrate that a significant number of human beings have responded to all His efforts to save them, including the ability, by grace, to keep His commandments. Thus Satan's charge that it is impossible to keep God's laws will be shown to be false.

Second, the investigative judgment *is* for our benefit. Although not physically present, Satan is our accuser before the judgment throne, as Zechariah 3 points out. Christ our Advocate represents us by assuming our sins, blotting them out of the records of heaven, covering us with His righteousness. After they have been sealed, God's people become "men wondered at." They perfectly reflect Christ's character and are used by the Holy Spirit to witness to God's love and glory in a world that has been longing for such a demonstration. This is the way—the only way—that His work can be finished on earth. The character of God will be fully reproduced in His people. See *Christ's Object Lessons,* p. 69.

A third benefit that those who question the investigative judgment seem to overlook is its benefit to the onlooking universe. The sinless beings who populate this universe have witnessed the inroads of sin in our lives. They cannot help but wonder whether we are safe to save—whether we are fit to join the sinless, unfallen hosts of the universe. As they participate in the investigative judgment they validate what God has known all along. As a result, they will be happy to accept the saved as joint heirs with them for eternity.

Undoubtedly God has many more good reasons for His investigative judgment. Although we may not fully understand all His reasons, that does not mean that He does not know what He is doing or that He was mistaken about announcing the hour of the investigative judgment in 1844.

Another question arises out of the teaching that the judgment is taking place in heaven now: What is the basis of that judgment? On what grounds are we to be judged?

Ellen White wrote in 1893 that "the day of final account will come, when the Lord reckons with His servants. The Chief Shepherd is Judge and illustrates the great principles which are to regulate the proceedings of the reckoning with His servants who are *justified by faith, judged by their works*. Faith works by love and purifies the soul of moral defilement that it may become a temple for the Lord."—*This Day With God,* p. 208, emphasis supplied. Christ illustrates the great principles involved in the final judgment by using the parable of the talents to demonstrate our accountability to God. Ellen White adds that this parable includes the concept of improving in *character* as well as in *ability*. She states: "The light of truth and all spiritual advantages are the Lord's gifts. They are to be appreciated and are to have influence upon the mind and character. We are to return to God corresponding increase, according to the gifts entrusted."—*Ibid*. God's greatest gift is the gift of His Son. That gift alone makes our salvation possible. We cannot earn it, and we do not deserve it. But we must realize that with its reception comes the responsibility of returning to God a corresponding increase. If we accept Ellen White's statement that salvation is God's greatest gift, we must conclude that, at least in this respect, all of us have received ten talents.

What, then is a "corresponding increase"? The former head of the General Conference Ministerial Association, Elder R. A. Anderson, used to put the answer this way: "Salvation is free, but discipleship costs us everything we have." Because God gave everything He had for our salvation, we must dedicate everything we have in return. When we accept the ten talents, we accept the responsibility of placing all ten of them—all that we are and have—on the altar of sacrifice, holding back nothing, making no reservations, clinging to no pet sins. To claim that we are justified without subsequently committing all we have and are to Christ is to deceive ourselves and to limit God's ability to make us the kind of people that He wants us to be.

What is God able to do in us? The good news is that God can accomplish far more in us and for us than the human mind considers possible. He is able to keep us from falling. See Jude 24. Christ's obedience while here on earth was not a substitutionary obedience but an exemplary obedience. He came to show us how, by His grace, we *can* overcome. "His practical example left us a plain pattern which we are to copy. . . . Not only did Christ give explicit rules showing how we may become obedient children but He showed us in His own life and character just how to do those things which are right and acceptable with God, so there is no excuse why we should not do those things which are pleasing in His sight."—*Selected Messages,* bk. 3, pp. 138, 139.

Christ showed us the way. He made it possible for us to follow His example, and He will judge us by that standard. "When He comes He is not to cleanse us of our sins, to remove from us the defects in our characters, or to cure us of the infirmities of our tempers and dispositions. If wrought for us at all, this work will all be accomplished before that time. When the Lord comes, those who are holy will be holy still. Those who have preserved their bodies and spirits in holiness, in sanctification and honor, will then receive the finishing touch of immortality. But those who are unjust, unsanctified, and filthy will remain so forever. No work will then be done for them to remove their . . . sins and their corruption. This is all to be done in these hours of probation. It is *now* that this work is to be accomplished for us."— *Testimonies,* vol. 2, p. 355.

"Do not be deceived: God cannot be mocked. A man reaps what he sows. The one who sows to please his sinful nature, from that nature will reap destruction; the one who sows to please the Spirit, from the Spirit will reap eternal life." Galatians 6:7, 8, NIV.

## Losing Is Not Earning

Although Adventists are sometimes accused of trying to "earn their way to heaven," I have never met a member of this church who subscribes to this position. What Adventists do teach, on the clear authority of Scripture, is that Christ's sacrifice alone makes it possible for us to be saved and taken to heaven. On the other hand some of the things we do *can keep us out* of heaven.

Malachi 3:5 is God's answer to the question of chapter 2:17, "Where is the God of judgment?" "Here I am," God says. "Right here near you, watching you, and taking into account what you are doing." The Lord goes on to outline some of the things He has witnessed and for which He will judge His people:

1. Sorcery
2. Adultery
3. False swearing
4. Oppressing the wage earner
5. Oppressing the widow
6. Taking advantage of the fatherless
7. Taking advantage of the stranger

This is not meant to be a full list. But it does mention some things that greatly displease God and for which we will be judged if we persist in them in spite of our profession of religion. This thought is repeated in other parts of the Bible. "There shall in nowise enter into it [the Holy City] any thing that defileth, neither whatsoever worketh abomination, or maketh a lie." Also left out of the city are "sorcerers and fornicators and murderers and idolaters." Revelation 21:27; 22:15, RSV. These evil acts keep people out of God's kingdom. There is a subtle distinction between the false idea that doing good earns entrance into heaven and the biblical teaching that doing evil keeps us out of heaven. We may not be able to earn heaven by what we do, but we certainly can lose the privilege of being there by neglecting to do what God tells us to do. Recognizing this fact will make a great deal of difference in how we practice our religion.

For example, Adventists should never keep the Sabbath in order to be saved. But when we fully understand what God is saying in commanding us to "remember the sabbath day, to keep it holy" (Exodus 20:8), we risk losing the heaven Christ has earned for us if we deliberately or carelessly ignore God's clearly expressed will in this matter. Why? Not because we disobeyed a direct command, but because behind overt acts of disobedience lies a spirit of self-will and distrust of God. We act out our conviction that God does not have our best interest in mind, and in so doing we violate both the law of the Sabbath and the natural law that stipulates that we need a Sabbath rest to insure good physical and mental health and proper spiritual development. This is not legalism. Every one of God's natural and moral laws were designed to meet human needs. We cheat ourselves when we violate any one of them, for we lose the best in life that God desires us to have. And that's a double loss. We lose heaven and we lose the blessings that come from obedience in this life. Those who disobey the fourth commandment lose the peace, joy, happiness, and preciousness of communion with God and the saints, and the physical healing and restoration of both body and mind that the Sabbath provides.

## "Everybody's Doing It!"

The attitude of the people in Malachi's day seemed to be, "Everybody's doing it, so it can't be too bad!" That same attitude lies behind so much of what we see happening today. As long as everybody's doing it, the modern mind sees no wrong in sexual promiscuity, impurity, dishonesty, cheating, or any other behavior that until recently was considered to be wrong.

In one sense, Jesus was the greatest crowd pleaser of all time. He was such a popular healer and teacher that it was difficult for Him to find time to spend alone with His Father and with His disciples. Yet He was never one of the crowd in respect to moral purity. He stands head and shoulders above everyone else who ever lived. His life demonstrates the opportunities that God makes possible for us. But His lifestyle was so different from that of the crowd that they ended up crucifying Him.

We who follow in His footsteps will be known by the company we keep. What a glorious privilege it is to be among the "crowd" that includes Jesus, Enoch, Joseph, Daniel, Paul, and John the beloved. In the light of where today's crowd is going, we certainly do not want to be swept along by the everyone-is-doing-it argument.

## "Return So That I May Return"

In a special way the so-called minor prophets carried God's

call to "return so that I may return." Hosea says, "Come, let us return to the Lord; for he has torn, that he may heal us; he has stricken and he will bind us up." Hosea 6:1, RSV. Why does God tear us? In order to heal us. Verse 2 expands this thought: "After two days he will revive us; on the third day he will raise us up, that we may live before him." The book of Zechariah begins with this plea: "Return to me, says the Lord of hosts, and I will return to you." Zechariah 1:3, RSV. Malachi 3:7 echoes, "Return unto me, and I will return unto you, saith the Lord of hosts."

But how did the stubborn people of Malachi's day respond? Just as you would expect by now, "Wherein shall we return," they asked in an injured tone. God mentioned something specific: they had been robbing Him. Of course they respond in horror at that suggestion. "Wherein have we robbed thee?" they asked. Verse 8. They had used for themselves the tithe and offerings that God claims as His. Notice that their crime includes stealing "offerings." We often talk about robbing God by withholding part of His rightful tithe. But the text tells us that our offerings are also His. He does not set a specific amount as He does in the case of the tithe. But if we are stingy and cringe when confronted with the offering plate and with the needs of those about us, we rob God just as much as by neglecting to turn in our tithe.

In the context of "return so that I may return" we learn that if we return faithful tithes and offerings God will return an even greater blessing to us. See verses 10-12.

### Mind Over Mutter

In verse 13 God calls on His people to account for their muttering and complaining against Him. Muttering is harmful to the body and mind as well as to the soul.

Dr. Solomon Snyder of the Johns Hopkins Medical School has come to be recognized as one of the world's leading authorities on the neurochemistry of the brain. The June 1980 issue of *Psychology Today* contains an interview with Dr. Snyder that presents an update on his research into a group of neurotransmitters found in the brain that are known as peptides. Less than thirty years ago, scientists were aware of only four neuro-transmitters. Since then two dozen or so have been discovered. Dr. Snyder believes that there may be as many as 200 neurotransmitter systems that influence our behavior. He pinpointed which brain cells receive enkephalin, a morphinelike chemical that relieves pain and improves moods. Recently he has worked with other brain chemicals that promise to be even more potent painkillers while being less addictive.

One of the fascinating bits of information from this interview is Dr. Snyder's discovery of how powerfully the mind can influence the brain and the body. For instance, a placebo can cause the brain to produce enkephalin which in turn can effectively block out pain. Dr. Snyder concludes that psychological processes can hasten or ward off disease. He believes that well-controlled studies demonstrate the validity of the mind-over-matter concept.

As the mind can control our physical problems to some extent at least, so it can control mental and emotional ones. The spirit of criticism and complaining is one of the most insidious disease-producing attitudes. Ellen White warns that the souls of those who scatter the seeds of dissension reap the bitter fruits of dissension. She adds that "it never pays to think of our grievances. God calls upon us to think of His mercy and His matchless love, that we may be inspired with praise."—*The Ministry of Healing*, p. 492.

If we practice mind over *mutter,* we will find that it is one of the best forms of preventive medicine. *The Ministry of Healing* adds, "Nothing tends more to promote health of body and of soul than does a spirit of gratitude and praise. It is a positive duty to resist melancholy, discontented thoughts and feelings."—Page 251.

But the Jews of Malachi's day even muttered about God's warning against muttering! "It is vain to serve God," they said. Verse 14. They acted as though God had played some great cosmological joke on them by the way He was dealing with them.

Some people even suggest that in the Old Testament God plays jokes on His people and that sometimes He is unjust and vindictive. It is true that the human terminology used to describe God in the Old Testament may sound harsh at times, but when taken in their entirety, the Scriptures portray a God who is perfect, and perfectly just, in all that He does. He loves and cares for His children on earth, and He does not play cruel jokes on them. However, sin and Satan do, and they lead us to think that God is the source of our troubles. One of the hardest things God faces is getting us to place the blame where it belongs—on Satan, or sometimes even on ourselves.

### The Simple Secret of Faith

The picture was not an entirely bleak one. Even in a time of religious halfheartedness such as that which Malachi describes, God had precious jewels who were faithful to Him. The last verses of chapter three particularly encourage those who face the pre-advent judgment. If we trust the Lord, our names and the righteous deeds He has helped us to perform will be recorded in His book of remembrance. Malachi 3:16.

The Jews of Malachi's time made it almost impossible to serve God and to be saved. But Malachi set the record straight by showing the *simple* secret of faith—a secret so simple that it resembles the simplicity of children.

Thomas Edison loved to play with his two children, Marion and Thomas, whom he nicknamed Dot and Dash. One day he made a toy for them, attaching a small figure of a man to a telephone diaphragm. When the children talked, the vibration of their voices made the figure jiggle as if it were sawing wood. This started Edison thinking. If his voice could create motion, why couldn't motion reproduce the human voice? That thought led to a hasty experiment. Reporting it in his notebook of July 18, 1877, Edison wrote, "Just tried an experiment with a diaphragm having an embossing point and held against paraffin paper moving rapidly. I shouted, 'hello' into it and when replayed . . . I heard a distant sound which, with a strong imagination, resembled 'hello.' . . . There is no doubt that I shall be able to store up and reproduce automatically at a future time the human voice perfectly."[1]

Believing that he could do better, Edison worked on improving his recorder. He tells us that "instead of using a disc I designed a little machine using a cylinder provided with grooves around the surface. Over this was to be placed tinfoil which easily received and recorded the movements of the diaphragm.

"A sketch was made. The workman who got the sketch and $18 piece work for the job was John Kruesi. . . . I didn't have much faith that the 'talking machine' would work, expecting that I might possibly hear a word or so that would give hope for the future idea.

"Kruesi, when nearly finished, asked what it was for. I told him I was going to record talking, and then have the machine talk back. He thought it was absurd."—*Ibid.*

The main feature of Edison's new recorder was a cylinder wrapped in tinfoil. A handle at the end of a shaft allowed the device to be turned. The voice was recorded through a diaphragm having an embossing point that cut a groove into the tinfoil. As the workers gathered around him, Edison, with his keen sense of showmanship, recited, "Mary had a little lamb. Its fleece was white as snow, And everywhere that Mary went the lamb was sure to go." When he played it back he was pleased that it reproduced so well. Edison reports, "Everyone was astonished. Kruesi turned pale and crossed himself. I was always afraid of things that worked the first time. Long experience proved that there were greater drawbacks found generally before they could be commercialized, but here was something that there was no doubt of."—*Ibid.*

After this amazing invention was introduced to the scientific community, one critic wrote, "It is so simple in its construction—not one whit as complex as the sewing machine—that one wonders why it was never discovered earlier."—*Ibid.*, p. 9. Edison's answer was that university scientists and technicians only saw "that which they were taught to look for" and therefore missed "the secrets of nature."

There is an important spiritual lesson here, for it is true in the spiritual as well as in the scientific realm that our perceptions are sometimes dimmed by preconceived opinions or false assumptions. Perhaps this is what Jesus had in mind when He said, "Verily I say unto you, Whosoever shall not receive the kingdom of God as a little child shall in no wise enter therein [the kingdom of God]." Luke 18:17. Edison's joy in frolicking with his children enabled him to bring himself down to their level and may explain his remarkable ability to look at things from a fresh viewpoint rather than from the viewpoint of biased presuppositions. Faith and finding the pathway to the kingdom of God are much simpler than philosophers and theologians recognize. Certainly the God who loves us makes it as easy as possible for us to find the way home to Him. It takes childlike confidence and willingness to accept what He tells us.

### Christ's Jewel Case

A note of triumph rings from Jesus' exclamation, "They shall be mine," in verse 17. He longs for us to be among those who make up His jewels. When we belong fully to Him we need not fear the investigative judgment. In selecting the jewels for His kingdom, Jesus does all He can to make sure that we will be among them. Did you know that God has a jewel case? Ellen White says, "The church of Christ is very precious in His sight. It is the case which contains His jewels, the fold which encloses His flock."—*Manuscript Releases,* vol. 1, pp. 236, 237.

Christ's church—His jewel case—contains many gems not yet fully polished that Jesus is preparing because He wants them to give special luster to His eternal diadem. As we explore His jewel case we discover some that already are formed into exquisite pins or brooches designed to hold His robe of righteousness in place. We notice many small, sparkling diamonds (small children in the church) that are particularly precious to Him. Some of Christ's jewels appear to be mounted in clasps that hold others close to His heart. There are even a few gold watches—their ticking alerts us to investigate what time it is on the prophetic clock. As we examine the jewels in Christ's case (His church) we find some that are damaged, but not beyond repair. Christ has commissioned the Holy Spirit to repair and restore them. There are jewels of all sizes, colors, and descriptions, and each one has been selected to complement and enhance the others. Each has its place in His collection, and He values each one for its uniqueness and beauty.

Of course, all analogies break down somewhere, as does this one. Every jewel case we have seen has been static and circumscribed by its original size. But Christ's dynamic jewel case expands forever. The more it increases in size, the more beautiful it becomes outwardly, as well as in the glory of its contents. The gems and jewels come to life through Christ's Spirit, helping to expand the jewel case. In fact Christ's jewels really are not the kind of jewels He wants them to be unless they are living jewels, actively expanding as they carry on His work. The growth God expects today requires an unusual expansion of effort and participation on the part of those already in the jewel case. But certainly such effort demands all that we can put into it in the glorious light of the many spectacular, sparkling jewels still to be added to Christ's jewel case.

### Why Don't We?
When Jesus longs so much to pour out His gifts of love and the Holy Spirit upon us, why don't we let Him do it?

Jesus was born in a manger that we might be born again to life eternal. He became human that we might become the sons and daughters of God. He lived in mud and squalor that we might live amidst riches beyond human description. He spent long nights in prayer that we might spend eternal days in the presence of God and the angels. He went homeless that we might live in the mansions He is preparing for us. Our precious Saviour trod wearily the dusty trails of little Palestine that we might skip with tireless feet along the streets of gold. He accepted in our behalf the crown of thorns that we might receive from Him crowns of gold. He died the death that was ours in order that we might live forever the life that was His. Why don't we love Him more than we do?

Our greatest need is a revival of true godliness among us. That revival *must* begin soon. It *will* begin soon. Ask yourself: Why not now? Why not with me? Why not?

1. Otto Wolfgang, "When Edison Invented the Phonograph," *NRTA Journal,* May–June, 1977, p. 8.

# CHAPTER 13

# Why Not Now?

If you could ask God a question what would it be? A little boy in Vacation Bible School recently responded to this query by writing, "Why do tigers bite?" His question is most perceptive. The boy lives in the Maryland suburbs of Washington, D.C., and perhaps had recently visited the National Zoo, where there are several beautiful tigers. Not long ago my family and I watched one of these tigers play with a small steel barrel. He stalked it as house cats do, knocking it into the water, then pouncing on it with a great splash and pushing it around the moat. The tiger obviously was having great fun with its toy. When we see these magnificent creatures acting playfully we cannot help but wonder, as the little boy did, why tigers bite. Of course, tigers do more than bite. Some of them become dangerous man-eaters that must be destroyed in order to keep them from killing or injuring more people. But why did the Creator, who made such beautiful beasts, provide them with the capability of causing such harm?

There is a much deeper and broader philosophic question involved. Why is there death and injury at all in God's universe? Why do people hurt each other? Why do they form armies and murder each other in the futile exercise known as war? Why do some good people, who live in harmony with the laws of life and health, die from cancer, whereas some cantankerous old "crab" who violates every principle of healthful living is still going strong at 100? These and many other such questions have long bothered those who believe in a good God who loves everyone.

In spite of the complexities involved, there is a simple answer. The loving Creator did not create an imperfect, dangerous, destructive world. All that came from His hand was perfect and good. The world as He created it was pleasant and peaceful. We cannot judge that original Eden by the sin that fills our present world. Why are there biting tigers, biting mosquitoes, and vicious people in the world today? Not because the Creator intended it that way. But a horrible cancer invaded God's perfect creation—the cancer of sin. We should not blame God for that. He did everything He could to prevent suffering and sin, except remove from human beings their freedom of choice. The inevitable results of rebellion and sin have now become all too evident in our world.

Some people deny that there is such a thing as sin. Yet they come face to face with it when they see animals kept behind bars and protective moats at the zoo. If people do not believe in sin, why do they carry keys? Why do they lock their houses and cars? The banker may not know much about the theology of evil, but he is fully aware of sinful human nature, and he takes every possible precaution to avoid being damaged by it when you ask him for a loan. On the other hand, we cannot imagine God creating this world without a solution to the sin problem. He has let sin run its course in order that the entire universe may see how devastating it is and refuse to ever let it rise up again. Once sin has been forever removed, the Creator's original plan for a perfect, happy life will be restored in this world. Tigers will not bite, nor will they be locked behind protective bars in zoos. See Isaiah 11:6-9.

### A Judgment Is Necessary

There must be a judgment in order for God to eradicate sin. Then, following the judgment there must be a carrying out of the sentences determined. This fact explains the no-nonsense beginning of Malachi 4. In His love God warns of the ultimate destruction of evil and those who persist in doing evil. There is no question about how this destruction takes place or about its results. Sin and sinners will be destroyed by a great blast of cleansing fire. See 2 Peter 3:10. Nothing will be left. The following sequence from Malachi 4:1 leaves no doubt about what will happen to the wicked:

1. They shall be stubble.
2. They will be burned up.
3. Neither root nor branch will be left.

But there is another side of the judgment that is much more pleasant to think about. The destruction of sin assures us of a "new earth, wherein dwelleth righteousness." 2 Peter 3:13. Malachi 4 also goes on to counterbalance the results of the judgment of the wicked with a glorious description of the blessed state of those whose names are recorded as jewels in the Lord's book of remembrance.

### "Kept in Heaven for You"

Peter's introduction to his first epistle rings with the good news that through Jesus Christ we have been designated the recipients of an "inheritance which is imperishable." 1 Peter 1:4, RSV. To this exciting prospect he adds the assurance that it is "kept" or "reserved in heaven for you." Verse 4. The use of the Greek perfect tense places an emphasis on the existing result of the completed fact—that the heavenly inheritance already has been reserved and is being actively safeguarded for us "where neither moth nor rust doth corrupt, and where thieves do not break through nor steal." Matthew 6:20.

This is a "living hope"—something we can count on. It is there. It is ours, made possible for us by the love and sacrifice of our dear Saviour. Yet often it seems unreal. Perhaps we need to cherish this living hope more than we do and meditate on it more often.

While sitting in a beautiful park in Healdsburg, California, in the summer of 1882, Ellen White felt a sweet peace come over her. She seemed to be taken away from this world. "The bright home of the saints was presented vividly before me," she reported in a letter to G. I. Butler, at that time president of the General Conference. "I seemed to be there, where all was peace, where no stormy conflicts of earth could ever come. Heaven, a kingdom of righteousness where all the holy and pure and blest are congregated—ten thousand times ten thousand and thousands of thousands—living and walking in happy, pure intimacy, praising God and the Lamb who sitteth on the throne! Their voices were in perfect harmony. They never do each other wrong. Princes of heaven, the potentates of this mighty realm, are rivals only in good, seeking the happiness and joy of each other. The greatest there is least in self-esteem, and the least is greatest in his gratitude and wealth of love.

"There are no dark errors to cloud the intellect. Truth and knowledge, clear, strong, and perfect, have chased every doubt away, and no gloom of doubt casts its baleful shadow upon its happy inhabitants. No voices of contention mar the sweet and perfect peace of heaven. Its inhabitants know no sorrow, no grief, no tears. All is in perfect harmony, in perfect order and perfect bliss. . . .

"Heaven, sweet heaven, the saints' eternal home, the abode for the toilers, where the weary who have borne the heavy burdens through life find rest, peace, and joy! They sowed in tears, they reap with joy and triumph. Heaven is a home where sympathy is alive in every heart, expressed in every look. Love reigns there. There are no jarring elements, no discord or contentions or war of words." Letter 30, 1882.

What an interesting and thrilling glimpse of heaven! As we read and contemplate descriptions such as this we feel eager to experience the joys of the inheritance kept for us in heaven. We also feel encouraged to persevere in the battle now going on. Life is not easy, but heaven is waiting for us.

Are you homesick for heaven? Do you long for its delights? Do you eagerly look forward to being with Jesus? In a sense we do not have to wait. We "can have a little heaven here below."—*This Day With God,* p. 271.

If heaven is so lovely, so desirable, why not bring it into our lives and homes right now? God has made this possible for us if we accept His will and let Him work it out in our hearts and lives. We may not be able to do much to change our outward environment. Fierce animals, fierce storms, and fierce people will still be about us as long as there is sin in our world. But by God's grace and power, we *can* change our inward environment—our hearts and our homes—and thus experience heaven in this life to a degree we have never considered possible.

The laws of life that God gave are designed to accomplish this purpose. As we cooperate with God's laws physically, mentally, socially, and spiritually, we find strength, peace, happiness, and victory that bring a foretaste of heaven even in this life. In our attitudes, characters, approaches to life, homes, work, churches, and service for the Lord, we can enjoy much more of heaven and the presence of Christ than we seem to realize *if* we are willing to lay self aside and let Christ take control of what we think, see, eat, drink, hear, study, say, experience, and do. Why settle for so little of heaven in this life when God makes possible so much?

## Preparation for the Day of the Lord

God does not force us to get ready now for the heaven to come. Ours must be a loving, willing commitment that involves remembering "the law of Moses my servant, which I commanded unto him in Horeb." Malachi 4:4. Christ's law is to be written so plainly on the tables of our hearts that in every act and word we will demonstrate our full commitment to Him.

Jesus warned, "As it was in the days of Noah, so it will be at the coming of the Son of Man." Matthew 24:37, NIV. We usually focus our attention on the crime, drunkenness, and immorality in Noah's day that seems so much like ours. But there is another comparison that we seldom think about. A few were accounted righteous enough, by God's grace, to go into the ark. At the forefront of this little flock was Noah. Ellen White records that "had he never lifted his voice in warning, his works, his holy character among the corrupt and ungodly would have been condemning sermons to the unbelieving and dissolute of that age. He bore himself with a Christlike patience and meekness under the provoking insults, taunts, and mockery. His voice was often heard in prayer to God for His power and help that he might do all the commandments of God."—*This Day With God*, p. 235.

As it was *in* and *with* Noah, so will it be in and with the little flock that is found in the ark of safety when the door of probation closes. God shut the door, not Noah. The door that shut

Noah in, shut the world out. Soon God will shut the door of probation, this time for the last time. Then the irrevocable pronouncement will be made as Heaven recognizes what exists in the hearts of every living individual: "He that is unjust, let him be unjust still: and he that is holy, let him be holy still." Revelation 22:11. After that pronouncement there will be no possibility of developing the kind of character that Noah developed by God's grace before entering the ark or that Enoch and Elijah developed before being translated.

Even those who profess to be Christ's followers today can be left outside when the door of probation is closed. Many of those who listened to Noah "professed to be worshipers of God. They claimed that their idols were representations of the Deity, and that through them the people could obtain a clearer conception of the divine Being. This class were *foremost* in rejecting the preaching of Noah. As they endeavored to represent God by material objects, their minds were blinded to His majesty and power; they ceased to realize the holiness of His character, or the sacred, unchanging nature of His requirements. As sin became general, it appeared less and less sinful, and they finally declared that the divine law was no longer in force; that it was contrary to the character of God to punish transgression; and they denied that His judgments were to be visited upon earth. Had that generation obeyed the divine law, they would have recognized the voice of God in the warning of His servant; but their minds had become so blinded by rejection of light that they *really believed* Noah's message to be a delusion. . . .

"But Noah stood like a rock amid the tempest. Surrounded by popular contempt and ridicule, he distinguished himself by his holy integrity and unwavering faithfulness."—*Patriarchs and Prophets,* pp. 95, 96, emphasis supplied.

It was not what was *around* Noah but what was *in* him that made the difference. By God's grace it will make the difference for us too.

### Reflecting Christ

God's last-day people will so fully reflect the "Sun of Righteousness" that the world will be attracted by the beauty of His character as it is seen in common people such as themselves. Then the hearts of the fathers will be turned to the children and the hearts of the children to the fathers. See Malachi 4:6. How can we today reach a generation for Christ that has been raised on the theory of evolution and is biblically illiterate? The best way is to show them that we are not sons of apes or sons of mud but sons and daughters of God. Then they will be pleased to turn to the religion of the fathers—those who truly knew Christ and attested to their full commitment to Him by all they did and said. Think of the final impact of 144,000 Elijahs, Noahs, Enochs, Daniels, and Johns on this last skeptical generation!

## Prescription for Revival

The details of what it means to be Laodicean are even more clearly spelled out in the first three chapters of Malachi than in Revelation 3. But the remedy, the prescription for revival, is outlined more specifically in Revelation 3 than in Malachi. So we turn to Christ's message to the Laodicean church for the specific answer to our greatest need.

Christ's love for us is so fervent that our halfhearted, lukewarm response cannot help but sadden Him. There were springs in Laodicea that bubbled forth hot water that mixed quickly with cold water to become lukewarm. Similarly, the members of Christ's last-day church have allowed the world to mix with the glowing, ardent heat that characterizes hearts animated by love. Yet while Christ is saddened by our attitude, He does not cast us aside. He knows all about us—not only what we are doing but why (see Revelation 3:15)—yet His words of loving rebuke are designed to draw us back into a living experience with Him. His fervent desire is that a change take place—that there be a true and lasting revival, a rekindling of the fires of the first love that will bring us quickly to the boiling point in our love and service for Him.

As the Great Physician, not only has He diagnosed our condition accurately, he also offers a prescription guaranteed to effect our complete healing. Christ's prescription, found in Revelation 3:18, is to be taken in three steps that perhaps can follow a reverse order to that which He used in describing them: (1) anointing the eyes with eyesalve in order that we might recognize our true condition; (2) removing our garments of sin and self-righteousness and clothing us with His white robe of righteousness; (3) receiving from Him an abundant supply of the gold of "faith that works by love." See *Christ's Object Lessons,* p. 158.

We must recognize our need before anything else can be done to heat up our Christian experience with the fires of revival. The spiritual blindness that Christ points out in verse 17 demands our first attention. "The eyesalve is that wisdom and grace which enables us to discern between the evil and the good, and to detect sin under any guise. . . . The divine eyesalve will impart clearness to the understanding."—*Testimonies,* vol. 4, pp. 88, 89. A famous eye powder was available in ancient Laodicea from practitioners at the school of medicine connected with the Phrygian temple nearby. The suggestion has been made that it was used principally to benefit the partially blind. If that is so, there is a parallel to the condition of today's Laodicean church. Our spiritual vision is not entirely gone, but living amidst the blazing light of revealed last-day truth, we only partially comprehend the significance of that truth and fail to recognize how much we lack the spiritual fitness necessary to have a part in sharing the truth.

Ellen White observes that "the 'eyesalve,' the Word of God, makes the conscience smart under its application; for it convicts of sin. But the smarting is necessary that the healing may follow, and the eye be single to the glory of God."—"Ellen G. White Comments," *S.D.A. Bible Commentary,* vol. 7, p. 965.

When applied properly, the eyesalve enables us to see both outwardly and inwardly what we have not recognized entirely in the past. Outwardly we behold as never before the glory and beauty of the spotless life of Jesus. Inwardly we see ourselves as we really are—sinners standing in need of the righteousness and saving power of Jesus. The Laodicean message diagnoses the condition of our spiritual health. It challenges us to allow the Great Physician to apply His remedies before it is too late. It is not yet too late to be revived and restored. But there is a note of urgency in our Physician's diagnosis. With all the concern and persuasiveness at His disposal, He urges us to arouse to action and receive the healing treatment immediately.

The Great Physician also says that we are naked and don't know it. He speaks, of course, of our spiritual nakedness. We are clothed with the filthy rags of our own righteousness and are in desperate need of His righteousness.

This parallels the attitude of the mythical emperor who was supposedly outfitted with beautiful clothing that he was unable to see. In spite of pretensions to the contrary, his subjects could not see his invisible garments either. In spite of our pretensions, our covering of self-righteousness also is invisible. It exposes our sins and rebelliousness for all to see. The shame of our nakedness (see Revelation 3:18) is that we seem unable to understand what everyone else recognizes about us. The remedy for our lack of perception was outlined in the first prescription—the eyesalve of the Holy Spirit. The work of the Spirit is to uplift the character of Christ before us and to reprove sin by applying the Word of God to our consciences. What can we do when we recognize that we lack the white raiment? Ellen White suggests the answer in the chapter in *Christ's Object Lessons* entitled "Without a Wedding Garment."

"By the wedding garment in the parable is represented the pure, spotless character which Christ's true followers will possess. . . . It is the righteousness of Christ, His own unblemished character, that through faith is imparted to all who receive Him as their personal Saviour.

"Only the covering which Christ Himself has provided can make us meet to appear in God's presence. This covering, the robe of His own righteousness, Christ will put upon every repenting, believing soul. . . .

"This robe, woven in the loom of heaven, has in it not one thread of human devising. Christ in His humanity wrought out a perfect character, and this character He offers to impart to us. . . . By His perfect obedience He has made it possible for every human being to obey God's commandments. When we submit ourselves to Christ, the heart is united with His heart, the will is merged in His will, the mind becomes one with His mind, the thoughts are brought into captivity to Him; we live His life. This is what it means to be clothed with the garment of His righteousness. Then as the Lord looks upon us He sees, not the fig-leaf garment, not the nakedness and deformity of sin, but His own robe of righteousness, which is perfect obedience to the law of Jehovah."—*Christ's Object Lessons,* pp. 310-312.

Instead of having "need of nothing" (verse 17), we have need of everything—everything that Jesus has done, is doing, and will continue to do for us. There is a sense of urgency in His appeal. He urges us to exchange our fig-leaf garments of self-righteousness for His white raiment of righteousness now. Soon it will be too late.

Fortunately for today's church, Laodiceanism is not an incurable malady. The Great Physician's three-step remedy is guaranteed to cure if we allow Him to apply it in the proper manner. But one more step must be taken before the remedy is complete—the gold treatment mentioned in Revelation 3:18. Generous gifts of gold will eliminate poverty in the material world. Heaven's gold eradicates spiritual poverty. "The gold here recommended as having been tried in the fire is faith and love. It makes the heart rich; for it has been purged until it is pure, and the more it is tested the more brilliant is its luster."—*Testimonies,* vol. 4, p. 88.

Frequently Ellen White uses the phrase "faith that works" to describe the result intended by the Laodicean message. She states that "the faith we are required to have is not a do-nothing faith; saving faith is that which works by love and purifies the soul."—*Faith and Works,* pp. 48, 49.

Love is the golden mirror of a genuine faith. It reflects the righteousness of Christ that fills us. If faith does not result in our showing greater love for God and those about us, it is not genuine. No matter what claims we make about righteousness by faith, if the works of love and righteousness are notably missing in our lives, the claim is false.

Gold is the third and ultimate ingredient in Christ's prescription for last-day revival. We can anticipate that in the Adventist Church there will be a false revival centering around a lowering of the standard of piety in the church. At such a time

Christ calls for Laodiceans to reach a new experience with Him—a revival of primitive godliness, a reflection of the love, beauty, and glory of the character of Christ. This is our greatest need.

Most people in the United States have medicine cabinets filled with prescription drugs that have become outdated and useless. Perhaps that is a good thing in view of the growing awareness that many drugs cause worse problems than those they are intended to cure! Nevertheless, it is senseless to pay for a prescription and never use it. It is particularly senseless for the Laodicean church to ignore the prescription that the Great Physician guarantees to be the sure and immediate cure for the malaise that is hindering His work on earth today. "Be zealous therefore, and repent," He urges. Verse 19. Someday soon the church will respond so fully to this call that history's greatest display of the love of Christ will be seen in our world. This revival and reformation will not cease until Jesus comes. Such a revival is our greatest need. It *must* come soon. It *will* take place soon. In the light of that fact, we must ask ourselves: Why not now? Why not with me? Why not?